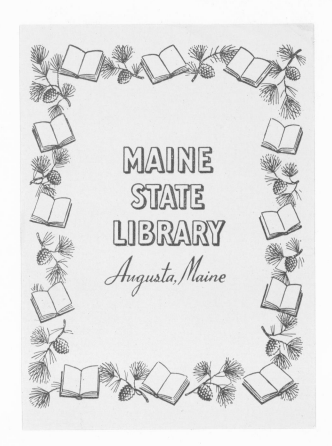

The British
Commonwealth
of Nations
in a Changing World

The British Commonwealth of Nations

in a Changing World

LAW, POLITICS, & PROSPECTS

Zelman Cowen

1964 ROSENTHAL LECTURES

Northwestern University School of Law

NORTHWESTERN UNIVERSITY PRESS

Evanston, Illinois

THE JULIUS ROSENTHAL FOUNDATION was established in 1926 to encourage preparation and publication of meritorious works of legal literature. Over the years the Rosenthal Lectures have been recognized as outstanding contributions to legal thought.

Julius Rosenthal (1827–1905), in whose honor the Foundation was established, was an eminent and beloved member of the Chicago Bar.

Copyright © 1965 by Northwestern University Press

Library of Congress Catalog Card Number: 65-12096

Printed in the United States of America

Preface

These lectures were delivered on the first three days of
April, 1964. Except for one or two cuts in the first lecture,
which were dictated by considerations of length, they are
printed in the form in which they were delivered. No altera-
tions have been made to take account of developments
which have occurred since the lectures were given. I have
thought it wiser to leave the text as it stood on April 3,
1964.

The subject of the lectures was chosen because it seemed
to me, in the aftermath of the Common Market debate of
1962 particularly, that there was much interest in the institutions of the Commonwealth in the United States. But
there was little knowledge and understanding of the evolution and development of the Commonwealth and its institu-

tions, and I attempted, as well as I could, to provide a sketch and a view primarily for American lawyers and law students. I have said little, if anything, which will add to the store of knowledge of the experts on the Commonwealth, but the response of my audiences at Northwestern encouraged me to hope that what I have written and said has made some contribution to their understanding and evaluation of the Commonwealth.

I was greatly honored by the invitation to deliver the Julius Rosenthal Lectures for 1964 and I should like to express my deep appreciation and gratitude to Dean John Ritchie and the Faculty of Law of Northwestern University. I should also like to thank Dean Ritchie and his faculty and students and others associated with the School for a memorable welcome and for their gracious and warm hospitality. My wife and I will not forget those very happy days.

ZELMAN COWEN

May 21, 1964

Contents

vii

I

The Emergence
and Definition
of the Commonwealth
# of Nations

IN THE EARLY 1960's a grand debate was in progress within the British Commonwealth. It had been generated by the decision of the United Kingdom to seek admission to the European Common Market. For the United Kingdom that decision represented a significant change of course. Only a few years earlier a Canadian writer on the Commonwealth had written:

> When [the British] are invited to strike out on another line of adventure and to throw themselves into the project of a Western European union, they shy away from it. British spokesmen always give as one of their main reasons for refusing integration into the European continent that their Commonwealth partners object to such a policy and that it would undermine their Commonwealth connections. But

> they have never quoted a leader from the rest of the Commonwealth to this effect. It is they who invite the Commonwealth to press them to stay out of European commitment, not the other Commonwealth nations who are doing the pressing spontaneously because of their concern for Commonwealth unity.[1]

It is one of the discouraging things involved in writing and talking about the Commonwealth that yesterday's statements and judgments date so rapidly. When that statement was written it was, I believe, a very fair representation of the British view. When, for reasons which appeared compelling to it, the United Kingdom government resolved to change course and to apply for entry to the Common Market, there was a sharp and immediate reaction in Commonwealth countries. From the older Commonwealth countries—from Australia, Canada, and New Zealand—came protests that British entry would adversely affect their economies and that important export industries would suffer in consequence of the loss of existing imperial preferences and of the extension of the European Economic Community's common external tariff wall to the United Kingdom. The point was made by political leaders in these countries that a decision by Britain in favor of the market was, in effect, a decision against her Commonwealth partners. India and Pakistan, which had become members of the Commonwealth in the immediate aftermath of World War II, pointed to the threat to their industries and economies, a threat made the more serious because of their desperate struggle for economic growth and development. Among the newest Commonwealth members, an African group rejected the offer of associate membership of the Community on grounds seemingly more emotional than substantial: it was said that this was neocolonialism and that it would retard their economic growth and diversification.

The substance of these various arguments is not the matter for present debate. A minister in the Australian government temporarily lost his political head for questioning them in the Australian context. The point is that the arguments were made insistently and sometimes shrilly during the course of the Common Market debates in 1962, and they were pressed when the Commonwealth Prime Ministers met in London in September 1962. The *London Economist*, a dedicated advocate of British membership of the Community, observed that the speeches at that meeting were not made by Commonwealth ministers to their colleagues so much as to the invisible audience back home. The Prime Ministers' communiqué very clearly reflected the divisions and the dispute; it summarized what another English journal described as the Commonwealth onslaught on the United Kingdom. But the communiqué also made clear the English intention to go ahead nonetheless.

There was another and subtler strand in the Common Market debate. This was formulated clearly and insistently by Sir Robert Menzies, Prime Minister of Australia, the most ardent and articulate of Commonwealth men. He said that the growth of the economic bonds of the Community would inexorably enmesh the United Kingdom in a political sense, that the logic of events would give political as well as economic shape to the Community; Britain would look increasingly to Europe, both economically and politically, and the Commonwealth would in the longer view dwindle into insignificance. It seems to me that there was force in this argument.

It is now history that this particular British bid to enter the Common Market failed. The British negotiators went back to Brussels to win the best available terms for admission, and they found General de Gaulle in the door. In the immediate aftermath of these events, questions were asked about the light they shed upon the character of the Commonwealth association. The *London Economist* wrote:

> . . . the Common Market negotiations have shown, simply by forcing some basic questions on the Commonwealth, that blood is not thicker than divergent interests and that a Commonwealth without institutions is not, and cannot be a unit. Even the alternative belief in the Commonwealth as the pointer to a multiracial world society of tomorrow has, to say the least, fallen into doubt.[2]

Another English writer put it that these events showed that the position of leadership in the new Commonwealth was more a matter of ritual than of substance.[3]

It is not an inappropriate time therefore to take another look at the Commonwealth, at the character and institutions, at the substance and shadow of the association. In choosing to do this before an audience of American lawyers, I shall give emphasis to matters of law and institutions, though ultimately I shall be concerned with broader questions affecting the significance and character of the association and its future.

II

The Commonwealth at the present time has eighteen member states: the United Kingdom, Canada, Australia, New Zealand, India, Pakistan, Ceylon, Ghana, Malaysia, Nigeria, Sierra Leone, Cyprus, Tanganyika, Uganda, Jamaica, Trinidad and Tobago, Zanzibar, and Kenya. They exhibit a variety of constitutional structures. The United Kingdom, Canada, Australia, New Zealand, Ceylon, Sierra Leone, Uganda, Jamaica, and Trinidad and Tobago are all monarchical; they severally acknowledge Queen Elizabeth as their sovereign. India, Pakistan, Ghana, Cyprus, Tanganyika, Nigeria, Zanzibar, and Kenya have adopted republican constitutions. Some years ago Ceylon gave notice that she would move towards republican status, but she has not yet done so. Malaysia is unique in having its separate monarchical structure; the Malaysian monarch is chosen for a term of years from among the rulers of the nine Malay states.

All the Commonwealth countries acknowledge Queen Elizabeth as Head of the Commonwealth, the symbolic bond of the association. All of them, with the exception of the United Kingdom, have one element in common: in one way or another they attained independence from a status of dependence of one sort or another—whether as a colony, protectorate, or trust territory—on the United Kingdom. The Commonwealth in this aspect has been somewhat colorfully characterized as a strange and fortunate grouping of nations originally created by the accident of a maritime colonialism borne on the trade winds.[4] A former British Secretary of State for Commonwealth Relations has written:

> The Commonwealth is not an artificial creation nor a club that can be joined; it is a natural unit and therefore has natural limits. It is made up of countries that have, for historical reasons, certain profound affinities one with another. Without the will and capacity to cooperate that spring from these affinities, the links of Commonwealth would become so vague and general as to be meaningless. It would not be enough, as is sometimes assumed, for a member country to have close natural links with Britain alone; to be a Member of the Commonwealth it would need to have similar affinities with India, Canada, Australia and all the other existing and future members of the Commonwealth.[5]

8

Burma, alone among the states granted independence since the end of World War II, elected to take that independence outside the Commonwealth. And that decision, it has been suggested, was taken in special circumstances. If Burma could have postponed her decision for a very few years until the changed character of the postwar Commonwealth had been exhibited by the accession of India, Pakistan, and Ceylon, her decision might well have been different. But in the immediate aftermath of the war, it was still assumed in Asia that independence outside the Commonwealth was bigger and better than independence inside it.[6]

Three other states formerly within the Commonwealth have ceased to be members. Ireland became a republic and formally seceded in 1949. The history of Anglo-Irish relations has been fairly described as "the great failure of British statesmanship in our day." [7] In the aftermath of bitter struggle, Ireland became a member of the Commonwealth, virtually by *Diktat*, in the early 1920's. In the years before World War II she progressively cut away her ties with the United Kingdom. Very tenuous relations with the British monarchy were maintained by an Act of 1936, and in 1937 a new constitution establishing Eire as a "sovereign independent, democratic state" was adopted with an elected President as its head. Ireland remained neutral during World War II and cut the last formal remaining ties in April 1949. The going-out was amicable, and the United Kingdom Act which acknowledged this event made special provision for the status of Irish citizens, who are not regarded in the United Kingdom and in some other Commonwealth countries as aliens.

The case of South Africa was different, and her withdrawal from the Commonwealth in 1961 was a reflection of tensions within the multiracial Commonwealth which had emerged in the years following World War II and which, it appeared, could not contain a country committed to extreme policies of apartheid and racial discrimination. We shall consider the South African withdrawal more fully later.

The third departure was of a rather different sort. In 1931, at the date of the Statute of Westminster, Newfoundland was a dominion—the term then used to describe Commonwealth members—for the purposes of that Act. But shortly thereafter Newfoundland ran into financial difficulties; in 1933 her dominion status was temporarily suspended, and in 1934 a special Commission of Government was set up. As Lord Attlee in characteristic style and with a little acidity relates, Newfoundland "was eventually obliged to surrender her sovereignty by the Conservative British government of the day rather as if she had been a defaulting Board of Guardians." [8] Further decisions were taken in 1946; a referendum was held in 1948 which produced a vote in favor of confederation with Canada; and in 1949 Newfoundland became the tenth province of Canada.

The word Commonwealth is well known to Americans. It

is the description and part of the title of a number of American states. For his classic book on the United States, Lord Bryce chose the title of *The American Commonwealth*. The word is also used to describe the present relationship between Puerto Rico and the United States.[9] In the American context Commonwealth has connotations of government based on consent and the partnership of citizens in the making of decisions.[10] And this is also its broad sense in the usage of the Commonwealth of Nations. It appears that the first British usage of the term, as applied to the states which became the Commonwealth of Nations, was in a speech in Australia by Lord Rosebery in 1884 when he described the Empire as "a Commonwealth of nations." In 1917, one of the greatest of Commonwealth men, Field Marshal Smuts of South Africa, in a speech in England referred to "the so-called Dominions, independent in their government [which] have been evolved on the principles of your free constitutional system into almost independent States which all belong to this community of nations, and which I prefer to call 'the British Commonwealth of Nations.' "

The usage took hold; Commonwealth was preferred to Empire to describe these particular states and their relations to the United Kingdom. When Smuts spoke in 1917, Canadian, Australian, New Zealand, and South African troops were fighting alongside United Kingdom troops in the various theatres of World War I. They had not been consulted about their participation in that war, though they participated willingly. As Andrew Fisher, the Australian Prime Minister, said of his country and countrymen in 1914, they undertook commitment to the last man and the last shilling. During the course of the latter part of the nineteenth century and early part of the twentieth, these countries had established a pre-eminent position among British possessions and had won from the United Kingdom a substantial acknowledgment of internal autonomy and self-government. At a conference held at London in 1907 they pressed for a new title in place of colony to describe their special position, and so was born the title of dominion, a title and description of status which was embodied in the Statute of Westminster and remained in common usage up to the time of the great post-1945 changes.

In 1947 the Indian Independence Act made provision for the establishment of two dominions of India and Pakistan, but by this time the title was démodé. The reasons were stated by Mr. Gordon Walker, a postwar Secretary of State for Commonwealth Relations, in explaining the reasons for the change of title of the United Kingdom governmental office concerned with Commonwealth affairs from the Dominions Office to the Commonwealth Relations Office.

The timing of this step was determined by the imminence of Indian independence, but it was at the same time due to the mounting desire of the old members to obliterate every formal distinction between themselves and the United Kingdom. In announcing the change Mr. Attlee said, "It has for some time past been clear that in certain quarters, both here and overseas, the view has been taken that the title of the Dominions Office is no longer entirely appropriate." Among the "certain quarters" was Canada. Shortly before Mr. St. Laurent had told the Canadian House of Commons of Canada's objections to the term "Dominion" which implied subjection.[11]

A new vocabulary is a reflection of changing attitudes. Even the usage of the term Commonwealth of Nations reflects difference of viewpoint; Australians and New Zealanders will customarily qualify it by the preceding adjective "British," but this is certainly not acceptable to the greater part of the membership of the association.

Few foresaw the extraordinary growth of the Commonwealth after 1945. And with that growth has come a profound change in the character of the association. In 1954, when the membership of the Commonwealth stood at eight, the Prime Minister of Pakistan in a speech at Lahore said:

Hitherto the Commonwealth has been an association of nations of European, largely Anglo-Saxon extraction. Culturally it was European, the indigenous populations of the dominion being totally ignored. English was the language spoken by the preponderant majority of its peoples. With the emergence of India, Pakistan and Ceylon as independent states, the character of the Commonwealth has undergone a radical change. The population of Pakistan alone (76 million) is more than the total white population of the Commonwealth. In addition India has over 350 million and Ceylon over 7 million people. It has thus become a multi-racial, a multi-cultural and a multi-lingual Common-wealth.[12]

The book summarizing the discussions of the unofficial Commonwealth conference at which this speech was made bore the title of *The Multi-Racial Commonwealth*, and this underscored what had become a critical issue of Common-wealth relations: whether an association profoundly trans-formed in this way, and through which the now celebrated winds of change were blowing violently, had meaning and capacity for survival. When terms were agreed to by the Commonwealth Prime Ministers in 1949 for India to main-tain Commonwealth membership, Mr. Nehru said that this brought with it "a touch of healing." At a later stage, just before Ghana became independent in 1957, Kwame Nkrumah spoke of the multiracial Commonwealth as a bridge between a colonial and a free association of nations:

> The Commonwealth can, I believe, become a pilot scheme for developing the most effective methods by which colo-nialism can be ended without revolution or violence and under conditions in which the former colonial territory still retains a close and friendly association with the former imperial Power.

During the last decade, the cultural, linguistic, and racial diversities of the Commonwealth have increased with each new admission to membership. Seven African states, led by Ghana in 1957, have become members. So too have Malaya, Cyprus, Jamaica, and Trinidad, each one adding to the diversity. There have been no additional "largely Anglo-Saxon" members, and the supply of potential candidates of this character is exhausted. With differences of race, language, and culture come differences of outlook and interest, and the remarkable diversification of the Commonwealth raises critical problems. Ultimately it raises the question of whether the association can survive as a meaningful and viable organization.

III

Many thoughtful Englishmen in the nineteenth century contemplated a day when the colonies would throw off the yoke of dependency and go their own way as independent nations. This was regarded as a natural evolutionary pattern; separation from the mother country, in Gladstone's words, was "a natural and beneficial result" provided, as he told the House of Commons in 1870, "that that separation so far from being effected by violence and bloodshed, might be the result of a peaceable and friendly transaction." But a new imperialism emerged in the last quarter of the century and in the early days of the twentieth century; its exponents were statesmen like Joseph Chamberlain, administrators and writers like Lord Milner and Lionel Curtis, and they had a vision of imperial federation, in which the Commonwealth would be organized into a federal structure. The United States was seen by them as a Commonwealth of Commonwealths, providing a broad blueprint for the organization of an imperial Commonwealth. But it soon became apparent that "imperial federation . . . was a horse that would not run." [13] The most that came out of the dreams of imperial federation was the system of imperial economic and trade preferences which for long were understressed, until, under threat of British entry into the Common Market, they assumed a rather sudden and urgent importance in the great debate over the future of the Commonwealth.

The opposition to proposals for imperial federation came largely from the overseas territories of the Commonwealth, and particularly from Canadian leaders like Laurier and South African leaders like Smuts. Canadian and South African leaders consistently and emphatically rejected close institutional ties, and a later generation of Commonwealth leaders from these countries reasserted the unwisdom of engaging in constitution-making for the Commonwealth which involved the fashioning of closer institutional machinery. The meeting of Commonwealth Prime Ministers in 1946 noted in its communiqué that the accepted and developing procedures for consultation furnished the Commonwealth with the most satisfactory constitutional machinery:

> While all are willing to consider and adopt practical proposals for developing the existing system, it is agreed that the methods now practised are preferable to any rigid centralized machinery. In their view such centralized machinery would not facilitate, and might even hamper, the combination of autonomy and unity which is characteristic of the British Commonwealth and is one of their great achievements.

It was one thing to oppose and reject proposals to provide constitutional and institutional machinery to bind the Commonwealth countries more closely, but quite another thing to insist that law and practice should be formulated in such a way as to give the maximum legal assurance of equality of status as between the United Kingdom and the self-governing dominions. Even on this question of the definition of the Commonwealth relationship, there were very real differences of opinion. In the United Kingdom, there were those who thought that there was much unwisdom and little regard for the lessons of history in seeking legal definition. In the debate in the House of Lords on the Statute of Westminster Bill, Lord Buckmaster, a former Lord Chancellor, warned that "you should avoid as far as possible putting a definition . . . of what the relationships may be into the unyielding form of an Act of Parliament. That is what this

Statute has attempted to do." [14] This view commanded considerable support in Australia and New Zealand. Mr. Hughes, the Australian Prime Minister, returned home from an Imperial Conference in 1921 boasting that he had soldered up the constitutional tinkers in their own cans. A similar view was expressed by Sir Robert Menzies as recently as 1942 when he spoke of the constitutional work of the 1920's and early 1930's, culminating in the Statute of Westminster, as "open to grave criticism," as a "grave disservice," and as a "misguided attempt" to reduce to written form what "was a matter of the spirit and not of the letter." [15] To the Canadians and South Africans the matter appeared very differently; and it may well have been that very different home situations, with diverse population strands, made it most important for Canadian and South African leaders to seek and insist upon definition of the relationship between the United Kingdom and the self-governing dominions in terms that made equality explicit.

It is interesting to compare the Canadian Mr. MacKenzie King's view with that of the Australian Menzies. Mr. King spoke of the Declaration of the 1926 Imperial Conference, to which I shall shortly refer, as comparable in constitutional significance with Magna Charta. History surely teaches that beauty lies in the eyes of the beholder. Canadian and South African pressure for constitutional definition had the support of the Irish Free State from the time that state unhappily joined the ranks of the dominions. And though some, and perhaps many, in the United Kingdom like Lord Buckmaster may have doubted the wisdom of the exercise, the British government showed itself very willing to cooperate fully in the work of constitutional definition and to use its legislative processes to bring the existing legislative framework as far as possible into accord with the demand for equality of status. Indeed, a United Kingdom committee started work on the task of constitutional definition a year ahead of the Imperial Conference of 1926, so that when that Conference assembled it was able to produce its declaration and resolutions in a comparatively short space of time. It is historically wrong to explain the result purely in terms of unfilial Canadian, South African, and Irish pressure on an unwilling and recalcitrant mother country.[16]

The Imperial Conference of 1926 produced a statement, known as the Balfour Declaration (named for the presiding officer, and one of two to bear that name), which is celebrated in imperial constitutional history. The heart of the declaration was its definition of the status and relationships of the self-governing communities composed of Great Britain and the dominions.

Their position and mutual relation may be readily defined. They are autonomous communities within the British Empire, equal in status, in no way subordinate one to another in any aspect of their domestic or external affairs, though united by a common allegiance to the crown and freely associated as members of the British Commonwealth of Nations.

The equality to which the Declaration made reference was equality of status, not yet of stature. In stature the United Kingdom towered over the dominions, which had not yet found their feet in international relations. But there were various respects in which the asserted equality of status was contradicted by law and practice. Between 1926 and 1930 general and special imperial conferences and committees considered these matters and made recommendations which were finally given effect, in part as law in the Statute of Westminster and in part in agreements and conventions reduced to written form both in that Statute and elsewhere.

It was said by the Appellate Division of the Supreme Court of South Africa in *Harris v. Donges*,[17] one of the great constitutional cases of our time, that

> . . . prior to the Statute of Westminster, the "mischief" as is clearly shown by the reports of the Imperial Conferences of 1926 and 1930, was that the Dominions were not in the eye of the law "autonomous communities within the British Empire equal in status, in no way subordinate to one another in any aspect of their domestic or external affairs." In law the Parliament of the United Kingdom was still supreme. The suppression of the mischief of the supremacy of that parliament was the prime object of the Statute of Westminster; another mischief was that it was not considered that a Dominion Parliament had any power to make

laws having extra territorial operation. Both these "mischiefs" were removed by the Statute of Westminster.

So too was the mischief of the Colonial Laws Validity Act 1865, which was also considered by the Court in *Harris v. Donges*. The Act of 1865 originally had a liberalizing purpose, but by the 1920's its operation was seen to be repressive and to assert dominion subordination to the United Kingdom so far as it provided that a dominion law inconsistent with or repugnant to United Kingdom legislation was *pro tanto* invalid. Not long before the Conference of 1926, a practical illustration of these mischiefs had been afforded by the case of *Nadan v. The King*.[18] The Canadian Parliament purported to abolish appeals in criminal matters from Canadian courts to the Privy Council. The Privy Council held the abolition to be invalid on two major grounds: first, the Canadian legislation was inconsistent with United Kingdom legislation authorizing appeals, and was therefore bad under the Colonial Laws Validity Act; second, since the Privy Council sat in London, there was an unauthorized exercise by the Canadian legislature of extraterritorial legislative power.

The Statute of Westminster dealt with these various problems. Of particular interest was the way in which it dealt with the legislative supremacy of the United Kingdom Parliament. In its preamble the Statute recited a convention, an "established constitutional position," that no law thereafter made by the United Kingdom Parliament should extend to any of the dominions as part of their law, otherwise than at the request and with the consent of the dominion. Then by section 4 in the body of the Statute it was declared that

> No Act of Parliament of the United Kingdom passed after the commencement of this Act shall extend, or be deemed to extend, to a Dominion as part of the law of that Dominion, unless it is expressly declared in that Act that that Dominion has requested, and consented to the enactment thereof.

This is not the place in which to embark on an extended discourse on the sovereignty of the United Kingdom Parliament, for it finds no home, little understanding, and great incredulity on American shores. But it will suffice to say that the doctrine asserts that there are no limits to the *legislative* sovereignty of the United Kingdom Parliament. It is a legal, not a *political*, doctrine, and its sources are to be discovered in seventeenth-century English political and constitutional history. In the context of the self-governing dominions a settled practice, a "strong and unbending" [19] convention, had been established before the enactment of the Statute of Westminster that the United Kingdom Parliament would not legislate for the dominions without their request and consent, and this was recognized formally by the recital of the convention in the Statute.

Much has been written about the devices adopted in the

Statute to fetter the power of the United Kingdom Parliament. The use of the double device of convention and legal form was said to redouble assurance. But could a sovereign parliament bind itself? Did not the law of sovereignty assert the power of the United Kingdom Parliament to undo what it had done in section 4 of the Statute? In *British Coal Corporation v. The King* [20] the Privy Council said that the formal legal answer to the latter question was yes. In that case the Privy Council held that, following the passage of the Statute of Westminster, the Canadian Parliament might now abolish appeals in criminal matters to the Privy Council. But it also said that as a matter of abstract theory, with no relation to realities, it was open to the sovereign United Kingdom Parliament to exercise its sovereign power to repeal the operative provisions of the Statute. However, when the South African courts considered this matter, in *Harris v. Donges*, a very different answer was returned. [21] It was stated as the unanimous view of the Court that

As a result of section 4 of the Statute of Westminster the British Parliament can no longer pass an Act extending to the Union "Unless it is expressly declared in that Act that the Dominion," i.e., the Union "has requested and consented to the enactment thereof." This provision has by necessary implication been amended by section 2 of the Status of the Union Act 1934 which enacts that no Act of the British Parliament passed after the coming into force of the Statute of Westminster "shall extend, or be deemed to extend, to the Union as part of the law of the Union, unless extended thereto by an Act of the Parliament of the Union." This emphasises that the only Legislature which is competent to pass laws binding in the Union is the Union Legislature. There is no other Legislature in the world that can pass laws which are enforceable by Courts of Law in the Union.

As the Court observed, the South African Parliament had added to the handiwork of the United Kingdom Parliament by enacting the Status of the Union Act 1934 and by inserting therein a requirement of legislative extension by the South African Parliament before a United Kingdom Act should extend to South Africa. But what the South African court said very plainly was that the Statute of Westminster worked a constitutional revolution, that it put an end to the sovereignty of the United Kingdom Parliament so far as South Africa was concerned, and that freedom once given could not be revoked.

In a recent Australian case, the Chief Justice of Australia, Sir Owen Dixon, said that an Act of the United Kingdom Parliament which on its face appeared to apply to Australia, though there was no Australian request and consent to its enactment, would not "perhaps," in view of section 4 of the Statute of Westminster, apply in Australia.[22] This was stated with caution and without elaboration, and it does perhaps point in the same direction as the South African view, though there is not much profit in building on a solitary word. But there can be no doubt that the South African view would be asserted by all the post-1945 members of the Commonwealth.

The Statute of Westminster was not amended or extended to apply to the post-1945 Commonwealth members. What was done instead was to make specific and appropriate provision in each Independence Act, starting with the Indian Independence Act 1947. It is interesting to trace out the provisions in these various Acts relating to the legislative authority of the United Kingdom Parliament. The Indian Independence Act of 1947, the first to speak of "independence" and of an "independent dominion," provided that a United Kingdom Act should extend to India or Pakistan only if extended thereto by the legislature of India or Pakistan. The Ghana Independence Act 1947 transcribed the provisions of section 4 of the Statute of Westminster. Later Acts do not provide for extension *at all*. The Nigeria Independence Act 1960, for example, provides that no further Act of the United Kingdom Parliament shall extend or be deemed to extend to Nigeria as part of the law thereof, and that from the appointed day the United Kingdom government shall have no responsibility for the government of Nigeria. It is the current and conventional wisdom that when independence is granted it is not for the United Kingdom legislature, with or without requests or consents, to concern itself with the affairs of independent countries.

The older Commonwealth countries would certainly regard themselves as no less independent, but on due occasions and without sense of compromising dignity or bending the knee, they have invoked the procedures of section 4 of the Statute of Westminster. For example, the New Zealand Constitution (Amendment) Act 1947 was passed by the United Kingdom Parliament in accordance with the procedures specified in section 4 and conferred a wider power of amendment of the New Zealand Constitution on the New Zealand Parliament than that legislature had formerly possessed. The British North America Act 1949 conferred additional power of amendment of the Canadian Constitution on the Canadian legislature. There have been United Kingdom Acts extending to Australia, enacted in accordance with the terms of section 4 of the Statute. In all these cases the initiative has invariably been taken by the Commonwealth country concerned and never by the United Kingdom Parliament, which has not purported to exercise any independent judgment. In no meaningful sense is there any derogation from independence in the use of United Kingdom legislative machinery for these purposes.

Some Commonwealth countries have been concerned with more than asserting their independence of the United Kingdom legislature; they have also asserted a principle of constitutional autochthony: an unlovely word chosen to mean "that their constitution has force of law and, if necessary, of supreme law within their territory through its own native authority and not because it was enacted or authorized by the parliament of the United Kingdom; that it is, so to speak, 'home grown,' sprung from their own soil and not imported from the United Kingdom." [23] The Irish were the pioneers of attempted autochthony in the 1930's, and there was a nice legal dispute as to whether they had succeeded in their aim. Nowadays the debate is arid; learned writers may debate the constitutional *grundnorm*, but it is idle chatter of a transcendental kind.

It was said, with reason, that the Statute of Westminster was an "act of transcendent constitutional importance." [24] But the limits of its operation were not always clearly understood. In *Harris v. Donges*, it was argued that a necessary consequence of the grant of independence by the Statute of Westminster was that the South African legislature should thereafter possess the sovereign powers possessed by the United Kingdom legislature. In *Harris* the issue was the validity of legislation passed by the South African Parliament sitting bicamerally and voting by simple majorities in each House. The South Africa Act 1909 required that such legislation be passed by a two-thirds majority of a single Chamber comprising the membership of both Houses. The legislation was held to be invalid; the Supreme Court unanimously held that while the Statute of Westminster unquestionably made South Africa sovereign in the sense that it was thereafter *free from* United Kingdom legislative control, the South African legislature must still respect the laws of its constitutional being as spelled out in the South Africa Act

1909. It was not an inevitable attribute of sovereign freedom from external interference that there should be internal legislative sovereignty in the United Kingdom sense. No one could assert that the United States was not a sovereign state, though it had no sovereign legislature.

The Statute of Westminster made use of the engine of the law to deal with inequalities within the Commonwealth which could most aptly be dissolved by such techniques. But this was not the whole of the matter. Wheare, in his fine study of *The Statute of Westminster and Dominion Status*, has observed that "the interaction of usage and convention with rules of strict law is a fundamental characteristic of the constitutional structure of the British Commonwealth," [25] and between 1926 and 1930, as well as formulating the legal rules which found expression in the Statute of Westminster, the Imperial Conferences and Committees formulated and recorded various agreements and conventions bearing on the relations between the dominions and the United Kingdom. There is no point in cataloguing all of these; one or two examples will suffice.

One matter was the position and appointment of the Governor-General of a dominion. This particular issue had been highlighted by a dispute between the Liberal government of Mr. Mackenzie King and the Canadian Governor-General Lord Byng, which came to a head on the eve of the Imperial Conference of 1926. In furtherance of the purpose of eradicating existing inequalities within the Commonwealth relationship, it was accepted and agreed that the Governor-General should stand in the same relation to his dominion government as did the monarch to the United Kingdom government. The Governor-General was the monarch's personal representative; he was not in any respect an agent of the United Kingdom government, nor should the United Kingdom government have any voice in his appointment, which should be a matter between the monarch and the dominion government concerned. These conclusions were finally hammered out in the midst of a sharp controversy in 1930 over the proposal to appoint a distinguished Australian, Sir Isaac Isaacs, as the first Australian-born Governor-General of Australia. Hitherto the practice had been to appoint a man from the United Kingdom, but the Australian government desired the appointment of a distinguished local man. In this respect Sir Isaac Isaacs certainly qualified. The son of migrant parents, and born in Melbourne in 1855, he had had a brilliant career culminating in his appointment as Chief Justice of Australia in 1930. The announcement of the Australian government's intentions provoked some opposition within Australia, not directed against the man but against the principle of local appointment. The King, George V, was strongly opposed to the nomination, principally on the ground that it was undesirable to appoint a local man, but finally, on the insistence of the Prime Minister, Mr. Scullin, who was in England to attend the Imperial Conference of 1930, he gave way and made the appointment. The issue was still unresolved while the 1930 Conference was in session, but the controversy made it urgent to formulate principles and this was done. Since then practice has varied. Australian and New Zealand appointees have, for the most part, come from the United Kingdom, while Canada's governors-general have latterly been distinguished Canadians. Practice in the newer Commonwealth countries has also varied. It has been suggested that cross-appointments among Commonwealth countries would promote symbolic Commonwealth bonds, but so far no action has been taken in this direction.

One of the conventional devices adopted to achieve equality in Commonwealth relations was the "neutralization" of provisions in the law of Commonwealth countries which were survivals from days when the United Kingdom exercised more stringent control over her colonial possessions. For example, there are clauses in the Australian Constitution which provide that certain bills passed by the legislature shall be *reserved* for the monarch's further consideration; others provide that the monarch may *disallow* legislation passed by the Australian legislature and assented to by the Governor-General. These make extraordinary reading in the mid-1960's, though they appeared in a different light at the very beginning of the century when the Constitution came into operation. Such clauses remain because it was settled between 1926 and 1930 that they should not in any respect authorize British governmental control

and surveillance over Australian laws; and since they remain
there without teeth, it is not for practical men, sure of the
substance of independence, to worry about the shadow of
servitude. Others, including among their number distinguished lawyers in other parts of the Commonwealth, may
be deceived. In one of the great postwar constitutional cases,
Federation of Pakistan v. Moulvi Tamizuddin Khan,[26] Mr.
Justice Cornelius, the present Chief Justice of Pakistan, in
the course of an elaborate review of the constitutional evolution of the Commonwealth, pointed to these provisions for
reservation and disallowance in the Australian Constitution
and also to comparable provisions in the Canadian Constitution (enacted in 1867) and said, "In the face of these provisions, it is obvious that these great countries can hardly be
called 'Independent Dominions.' Their principal legislatures
work under controls imposed from without by force of
law." To this the quiet reply must be returned: not so, the
form is confused with the reality. It may be that this Pakistani view points to a significant difference in the attitudes of
Commonwealth countries to the *definition* of the Commonwealth relationship. It is *written* that India and Pakistan and
the more recent Commonwealth members are *independent*;
it is nowhere so written that the earlier members are independent. Maybe for some, and for reasons that are not too
difficult to understand, it is vital that independence be as-
sured in the form as well as in the substance.

Let me turn to an aspect of Commonwealth relations of

special interest to lawyers. Lord Attlee has recently deplored the passing of the Privy Council appeal.

> It is, I think a pity, because while one of the great binding ties throughout the British Commonwealth is a common respect for the rule of law, and especially respect for the British common law, a supreme tribunal on which sat judges of the highest distinction from the various countries of the Commonwealth was, I think, a matter of some importance.[27]

Some English and Commonwealth lawyers would agree, though I should not. The appeal to the Privy Council has a long history. It was defined and organized by Acts of the British Parliament in the first half of the nineteenth century and by later legislative instruments. Until late in the nineteenth century, the Bench of the Privy Council was composed exclusively of English judges. Later legislation allowed for a broadening of its membership, but it was only very recently that a more thoroughgoing attempt was made to draw into the service of the Privy Council the wealth of Commonwealth judicial talent. But even so a question remains as to the justification of the appeal. Why should it be necessary or desirable to preserve appeals which are costly, which involve expensive travel, and which involve reference of questions to a Bench which is generally physically far distant and often far distant in expert knowledge and experience? There can be little doubt that the Privy Council appeal had value in another day as a guarantor of due process of law in the broadest sense, and as a supervisor, encourager, and educator of colonial benches. In some cases, even at present, it may provide strength. But where Commonwealth benches are strong and confident in their strength, the survival of the jurisdiction is better explained as historic survival than as a matter of present need.

In the latter part of the nineteenth century there was a Canadian move to restrict the appeal, and the Australian constitution-makers in the last decade of the century wished as nationalists and rationalists to impose severe restrictions on it. As Isaac Isaacs said, a few years later, of the Privy Council, "It is a venerable body, and it sits in a somewhat dingy den in Downing Street." But the Australian proposals to restrict the Privy Council jurisdiction ran into formidable and vehement opposition in the United Kingdom. It was said that this was a wanton assault on the structure of Empire. The outcome was a compromise which gave the Australian High Court control over the determination of most distinctively federal constitutional questions. The general question of the appeal was taken up at an Imperial Conference in 1907 when it was proposed that an Imperial Court of Appeal to deal with United Kingdom and overseas appeals should be organized. Nothing came of this, and the Conferences of 1926–1930 did not carry the matter much further beyond recording that the maintenance of the Privy Council appeal was, so far as the United Kingdom government was concerned, "to be determined in accordance with the wishes of the part of the Empire primarily affected." Thereafter Canada abolished criminal appeals and at the outbreak of war was taking steps to abolish other appeals. The validity of this latter legislation was sustained by the Privy Council in 1947, and its statement of principle in that case reflects very clearly the contemporary attitude to problems of Commonwealth relations.[28]

It is not consistent with the political conception which is embodied in the British Commonwealth of Nations that one member of that Commonwealth should be precluded from setting up, if it so desires, a Supreme Court of Appeal having a jurisdiction both ultimate and exclusive of any other member. The regulation of appeals is . . . a "prime element in Canadian sovereignty" which would be impaired if at the will of its citizens recourse could be had to a tribunal, in the constitution of which it had no voice. It is . . . irrelevant that the question is one that might have seemed unreal at the date of the [Canadian Constitution]. To such an organic statute, the flexible interpretation must be given which changing circumstances require, and it would be alien to the spirit, with which the preamble to the Statute of Westminster is instinct, to concede anything less than the widest amplitude of power to the Dominion legislature.

There had been a good deal of dissatisfaction in Canada with the performance of the Privy Council in constitutional matters, and, during the 1930's, not a little anger. So far as South Africa was concerned, a Roman-Dutch system of jurisprudence found little reason in an appeal to a tribunal with small knowledge or experience of that system. South African appeals were few, and the Privy Council appeal was formally abolished in 1950. It is gone in India and Pakistan which had been a great source of business for the Privy Council. It has been abolished in some of the African Commonwealth countries, though it survives in Malaysia in a new guise. There, the Privy Council acts for and reports its decisions to the Malaysian Head of State, so that it is old wine in a new bottle. In Australia, the appeal survives and continues in non-constitutional and in rare constitutional cases. Some Australians, of whom I am one, believe that it should be abolished on the ground that it is an expensive and anomalous historical survial. But there is little urgency about the matter, and there is no Australian professional or governmental disposition to do anything to abolish it.

In recent years there has been talk of a reconstruction of the Privy Council, to give it a broader Commonwealth character and to make it peripatetic so that it will do its work in various Commonwealth countries rather than only in London. It has also been suggested at times that a Commonwealth Privy Council might aptly serve as a tribunal or arbitrator in disputes and controversies between Commonwealth countries. I do not think that the latter proposal lies within the realm of practical politics, and at the present time it seems to me that there is little to be said for a Commonwealth tribunal for other legal matters. The Commonwealth association does not, in my view, gather strength in this way; new institutions should have a rational base, and it is hard to see the case for this one beyond a somewhat sentimental desire for the retention of an institution, appropriately refurbished. I should prefer to say with Lord Normand, a recent member of the United Kingdom and Privy Council judiciary, that "the final accomplishment of its [the Privy] Council's] task ought therefore to lead to its own honorable extinction." [29]

I have spoken of this matter at some length because it may have a special interest to American lawyers. If I may be permitted a personal reminiscence: I recall that on a short visit to the United States some three years ago, when I was returning to Australia after participating as counsel in a Privy Council appeal, I encountered some incredulity when I explained that appeals in some cases were still taken from Australian courts to a tribunal in London. There was little heart in my explanation. Although it does not have a very fresh or a very great impact, I share the incredulity.

By 1939, at the outbreak of World War II, a good deal had been done to give constitutional shape and definition to the Commonwealth association. No one then foresaw the profound structural changes of the postwar era. Useful work had been done by the constitutional tinkers both for those who had wanted definition of the Commonwealth relationship and for those who had not wanted it. Among other principles which had been formulated, it had been declared that the autonomy of Commonwealth countries extended to the conduct of foreign and external relations. And in those days, as I well recall, an arid debate went on as to the precise meaning of the Balfour formula. Did the freedom of association carry with it freedom to secede? Did the autonomy and equality of the association carry with it a privilege of non-commitment and non-involvement in Britain's war? No formal answer was given to the first of these questions until after the war, though Ireland's relations with the Commonwealth from the mid-thirties on were very tenuous. But the outbreak of war in 1939 gave an answer to the second question. To Sir Robert Menzies the answer was simply that the King was at war, therefore Australia was at war; and that was also the view of New Zealand. But the Canadians made a separate and later declaration of war, and South Africa came in only after a sharp debate in which Smuts finally carried the day. Ireland remained neutral throughout. Of the problem, therefore, it could be said, *solvitur ambulando*; it was answered by the facts.

II

The Multiracial
Commonwealth:
Redefinition
and Adjustment

I T HAS BEEN WELL SAID that the rules and conventions which are traced and identified by one generation of lawyers as being the real roots of the Commonwealth have an awkward habit of withering away in the next.[1] It was certainly the unquestioned assumption of the pre-1939 Commonwealth that acceptance of allegiance to the Crown was an indispensable element in Commonwealth membership. The Balfour Declaration in 1926 spoke of the Commonwealth as "united by a common allegiance to the Crown," and one of the conventions recited in the preamble to the Statute of Westminster declared that inasmuch as the Crown was the symbol of the free association of the members of the Commonwealth, and as they were united by a common allegiance to the Crown, it was in accord with established constitutional practice that any law touching the succession to the throne or the royal style and titles should require the assent of all the Commonwealth parliaments. The fact that this was deemed to be of sufficient importance to be included as one of the two conventions expressly recited in the Act reflects the significance of common allegiance to the Crown in the constitutional thinking of the time. The rules were unexpectedly put to the test by the abdication crisis of 1936, and at that time the British Prime Minister, Stanley Baldwin, spoke of the Crown as the "last link of Empire that is left." The steps then taken by Ireland showed how tenuous had become Irish connection with the monarchy, but in a formal sense the link remained and Ireland did not become a republic until 1949.

Ireland at that time became a republic *outside* the Commonwealth. The Indian decision to establish a sovereign independent republic posed for the first time the question of whether the abandonment of allegiance to the Crown was compatible with Commonwealth membership. For India, the monarchy did not have the significance it possessed for most, anyway, of the older Commonwealth members. India had struggled for and had asserted *independence*; her leaders, as Lord Attlee reminds us, were the first of a line to have languished in the King's jails as a price for their political leadership in the independence struggles. When India became independent and set about the task of constitution-making, there was an internal division over the issue of Commonwealth membership. Certainly such membership was only acceptable on terms that India should be a republic, and it was a question whether this was compatible with the constitutional doctrine of the Commonwealth. An affirmative answer was given to this question at the Commonwealth Prime Ministers' Conference in 1949. The communiqué stated that India would continue her membership as a "sovereign independent republic," and the government of India announced its "acceptance of the King as the symbol of the free association of its independent member nations and as such the Head of the Commonwealth."

This was the agreement which, as Mr. Nehru said, brought with it a touch of healing. It doubtless also caused some unhappiness and discomfort to certain of the Prime Ministers who went along with it. Sir Robert Menzies expressed the fear in 1950 that the substitution of structural variety for structural unity carried with it the danger that the Commonwealth might degenerate into a purely functional association. In a group of independent states with diverse interests and outlooks, this danger was present anyway, but the liquidation of structural links made it all the more naked. However, it is clear that all the Prime Ministers judged that the price for continued Indian membership was worth paying.

The 1949 agreement has been called the "most spectacular event in the constitutional evolution of the modern Commonwealth." [2] It certainly was a major event and there can be little doubt that it "would have seemed outrageous to most of the theorists of the Commonwealth at the time when the Statute of Westminster was actually passed." [3] The terms of the 1949 agreement were not general; they concerned only India. But it was unthinkable that when Pakistan in turn converted to a republican form of government a different decision would be reached. So in 1955 both Pakistan and Ceylon were declared to be acceptable republican members of the Commonwealth. Ceylon has not yet taken the step. Ghana, Cyprus, Tanganyika, Nigeria, and Kenya have all been accepted as Commonwealth republics. The case of South Africa was special. She asked the Commonwealth Prime Ministers whether, if a projected referendum favored a republic, she might continue her membership on these terms. The answer was that the question was hypothetical and that it should be asked when and if South Africa decided to become a republic. The vote was held and it favored a republic. Thereupon, in 1961, South Africa renewed her application, but withdrew it in face of strong criticism of her race policies.

Generally, however, it is clear that republican status is compatible with Commonwealth membership. But the rule of association appears to be that if a member proposes to become a republic and wishes to remain a member of the Commonwealth, it must renew its application for membership on those terms. There is no continuance of membership as a republic without formal acceptance of the changed status of the member by the existing membership. And it is required of the republican members of the Commonwealth that they accept the Crown as the external symbol of the association and as such the Head of the Commonwealth.

Institutional diversity goes further; just as a republican status is acceptable, so too is a separate monarchy. This is Malaysia's contribution to the constitutional mosaic; her King, since 1957, is one of the Malay native rulers who holds office as Head of State for a term of years. In common with all other members of the Commonwealth, Malaysia acknowledges the Crown—Queen Elizabeth—as Head of the Commonwealth.

There has also been some change in the definition of the monarchical relationship in those countries which retain the British Crown as an integral part of their governmental structures, for they have done so on terms which connect the monarch specifically with each of them. It was agreed by the Commonwealth Prime Ministers at their meeting in December 1952 that the time was ripe for redefinition of the royal titles, and it was agreed that each Commonwealth country should devise its own appropriate form. So Queen Elizabeth has been proclaimed by different titles in the various Commonwealth countries of which she is Queen.

Where does the monarchy now stand in the Commonwealth? As late as 1952, Sir Winston Churchill asserted in indisputably Churchillian terms that "the Crown has become the mysterious link, indeed I may say the magic link, which unites our loosely bound but strongly interwoven Commonwealth of Nations." Attitudes to the monarchy are complex but most would say that Churchill's statement is very much overdrawn. Indeed, without disparaging its symbolic and historic utility, I think it is fair to say that a cooler and much less romantic, and sometimes perhaps even a critical, view is taken of the monarchy, or at least of some of its less attractive surrounds.

Commentators on the Commonwealth declaration of 1949 have spoken of it as "the despair of constitutional theorists," [4] as "almost metaphysical in its refinement." [5] But it had the great merit of accommodating forms to the practical realities of politics. The sacrifice of structural unity was the necessary price of housing a very different new membership which insisted on independence in fact *and* in form. And the contemporary law of the Commonwealth asserts that for various purposes Commonwealth countries are not to be distinguished from foreign countries. In *Government of India v. Taylor*,[6] the English courts rejected an argument that the government of India might enforce a tax claim in an English court, notwithstanding the general rule that those courts would not enforce *foreign* tax claims. As Lord Simonds put it:

It was argued that, whatever might be the position as between this country and a foreign country, it was not the

same as between different members of the British Commonwealth including those members which, though within the
Commonwealth, did not acknowledge the sovereignty of
the Queen. For such a distinction there is no authority, and
I can see no reason.

There was no dissent from this proposition by any of the
judges. It may be that there is good practical sense in the rule
as stated by Lord Simonds, though I do not see its merits
quite so clearly in a Commonwealth which lays stress on the
values of cooperation. This rule, in any event, appears to
antedate the modern developments in the Commonwealth,
for rather more than fifty years ago an English court held
that an Australian municipal corporation could not enforce a
tax liability in England.[7] But the *Taylor* case was a very
specific assertion of the rule by the highest English court,
which was called on to consider the matter in light of the
Commonwealth relationship. Another rule of law which
assimilates Commonwealth and foreign countries is the
doctrine of the immunity of sovereign states in English and
other Commonwealth courts. Nothing turns on the constitutional structure of the Commonwealth country which it is
sought to implead; the rule is the same whether it is a
monarchy, a special monarchy, or a republic.[8]

Indeed, survivals in the law, which make distinctions between foreign and Commonwealth countries and which do
not take account of the evolution of the Commonwealth,

may prove to be very unsatisfactory. The case of surrender for trial in another country aptly illustrates this point. In extradition treaties between foreign countries, the return of persons to stand trial for political offenses is normally excepted. When in 1963 a man was returned by the United Kingdom to Nigeria to stand trial on political charges, there was a very sharp debate in England. The government defended its action on the ground that the Fugitive Offenders Act, under which it acted, did not allow of such an exception. That Act was framed for a very different, colonial situation, and if for purposes of judicial interpretation the Nigerian case fell within its terms the time was surely ripe for amendment of the law to take account of the fact that Commonwealth countries are now independent polities with independent policies.[9]

If a short digression, a frolic of my own, is momentarily permitted, I may observe that the cases occasionally turn up some interesting and rather elaborate discussions of Commonwealth questions in unlikely and unsuspected places. The status of Ghana fell to be discussed in a case which points up a surviving distinction in English statute law between Commonwealth and foreign countries. In *Gohoho v. Guinea Press, Ltd*,[10] the pregnant question was whether a writ or notice of a writ should be served in Ghana in legal proceedings instituted in England. Behind this technical question lurked some history and diplomatic nicety. In the nineteenth century, when the rule was devised, it was regarded as an offense to the dignity of a foreign country to serve the English monarch's writ within its territory; in such a case, therefore, only notice of the writ was to be served. It was otherwise if the territory was subject to British control. But Ghana had been independent since 1957, and a republic since 1960. Nonetheless, and without too much affront to dignity it is hoped, Ghana was held to fall within the definition of the "British dominions" for the purpose of the rule. Still on the frolic, and in a minor key, it may be added that high questions touching the evolution and development of the Commonwealth sometimes fall to be considered by judges in unlikely jurisdictions and in unlikely contexts. For example, in construing an investment clause in a settlement made in 1936, an English Chancery judge had to decide whether a power to invest in the public stocks or government securities of any British colony or dependency authorized investment in Canadian securities. The judge carefully considered the terms of the Balfour declaration of 1926, the Statute of Westminster, and the Privy Council decision in *British Coal Corporation v. The King*. His conclusion was that the investment clause was not apt to authorize investment in Canadian stocks. "I cannot see how states equal in status and in no way subordinate to one another can possibly be said in any respect to be dependent one upon another." [11]

All of which goes to show that we must not neglect any source to discover the constitutional law of the Commonwealth. But to return to the mainstream, important legal questions relating to the Commonwealth fell to be considered in the immediate post-1945 period. Such a matter was the law of nationality and citizenship. The earlier doctrine was that there was an undifferentiated status of British subjects; no more precise designation existed to identify or connect a person with a particular Commonwealth country. Yet, anomalously, a person naturalized as a British subject in Australia, pursuant to the provisions of Australian law, who had taken the oath of allegiance to the King in Australia, was held to be an alien in the United Kingdom on the ground that such a naturalization had only a local operation.[12]

In a Commonwealth in which the individual members, other than the United Kingdom, played little, if any, independent role in international affairs, such an undifferentiated status worked not too badly, though it was necessary for certain purposes to devise a working notion of separate nationality for Commonwealth countries. For example, such a notion was accepted to qualify Commonwealth nominees for membership of the Bench of the Permanent Court of International Justice. The rule that there could be only one judge of any particular nationality did not exclude an Australian judge if there were already a United Kingdom judge on the Court.

The Imperial Conferences of 1926–1930 considered questions of nationality and citizenship. The propriety of formulating separate bodies of nationality and citizenship law for individual Commonwealth countries was accepted, and it was also said to be desirable to preserve and secure a common status connecting and associating all the nationals and citizens of individual Commonwealth countries.

In 1946 Canada took the lead in defining a separate Canadian citizenship; that law also declared that all persons who were British subjects under the law of any other Commonwealth country should be recognized as such in Canada. This was followed by a Commonwealth conference on nationality and citizenship which was held in London in 1947. The scheme recommended by that conference provided for the definition of individual bodies of Commonwealth citizenship law; it also contemplated provision for the preservation of a common status. The reasons for now defining separate nationalities and citizenships were stated in the report of the 1947 conference. Such a definition gave

> a clear recognition to the separate identity of particular countries of the Commonwealth, [clarified] the position with regard to diplomatic protection and [enabled] a Government when making treaties with other countries to define with precision who are the persons belonging to its country and on whose behalf it is negotiating.[13]

Also, by this time Commonwealth countries had a very different and more confident view of their own separate standing in the world. The plan adopted by the United

Kingdom and by some other Commonwealth countries was substantially in accord with the proposals of the conference, and that scheme was seen to have the merit of providing both a distinctive citizenship *and* a common bond or status. Not all the members of the Commonwealth made provision for the common status, but there is no Commonwealth country which regards a "British subject" wholly as an alien.

Long before these separate bodies of nationality and citizenship law came into existence, the rights and burdens of British subjects in other Commonwealth countries were already largely the creatures of local law. Specific provision might be made allowing British subjects *generally* (as contrasted with aliens) to practice professions, to exercise rights of franchise, and so forth; but these and other important matters, such as migration and residence rights, were defined and regulated by local laws. Until 1962 the most liberal practice, not surprisingly, was that of the United Kingdom, but the Commonwealth Immigrants Act 1962 for the first time restricted the right of free migration of British subjects or Commonwealth citizens into the United Kingdom. It was apparent that these restrictions were imposed because of the flow of unskilled colored migrants into the United Kingdom from other Commonwealth countries. The decision to impose these restraints provoked searching and sometimes angry debate: the *London Times* said that it "struck at the very roots of British tradition and Commonwealth links" [14], and in another leading journal of opinion it was said that the proposed law "drove a long nail into the coffin of the old Commonwealth." [15] That there should have been such sharp and emotional criticism is not surprising. Britain was the heart of the Commonwealth and had worked hardest at preserving it; and it is a bitter thing to abandon a cherished and liberal policy.

Indeed, immigration policies have not infrequently been a source of unhappiness in Commonwealth relations. The White Australia policy—the administrative rule adopted under authority of a colorlessly framed general law, which severely restricts non-white migration into Australia—is long-established and settled Australian dogma. A German, a Scandinavian, or an Italian finds it very much easier to gain admission as a migrant to Australia than does an Indian, a Pakistani, a Malay, a Commonwealth Chinese, or a West Indian. Australia does not stand alone in imposing such restrictions. In some Commonwealth countries, special restrictions have at times been imposed on British subjects of Oriental origin lawfully resident there. One of the bitterest sources of dispute between India and South Africa, at a time when the latter was still a member of the Commonwealth, was the discriminatory treatment of Indians resident in South Africa. In one notable case, *Regazzoni v. K. C. Sethia (1944) Ltd.,*[16] the English courts had to deal with a contract dispute in which the major point at issue was the recognition to be given to an Indian law prohibiting commercial dealings between India and South Africa. India also raised the matter of the treatment of Indians in South Africa as an international complaint in the General Assembly of the United Nations. While South Africa furnished the most conspicuous evidence of such discrimination, she by no means stood alone, and it is not surprising that discriminations against other Commonwealth citizens should have provoked resentment and anger. The response to such discriminations in some Commonwealth countries, such as India, was to provide by law that the grant of any rights to British subjects from other Commonwealth countries should be discretionary, and should be conceded on a basis of reciprocity.

It is a fair conclusion, then, to quote from two recent writers that

> . . . rights flowing from the common status remain on a precarious basis. Any government of a Commonwealth state, in the absence of an applicable treaty, may unilaterally, and even arbitrarily, modify operations of such rights. Citizenship laws in which there are references to the common status are subject to repeal or alteration. Thus, while the idea of a common status has survived in the concept of British subject or Commonwealth citizen, practice of the Commonwealth states in their relations inter se has caused it to be less meaningful than was the older Imperial concept of British subject.[17]

In a significant sense, this chapter of the law and practice of Commonwealth countries in their relations *inter se* throws a

revealing light on the contemporary Commonwealth association.

II

What rules determine admission to membership, withdrawal, and expulsion from the Commonwealth? One certain answer may be given: any member may freely secede. I
have already referred to the debate on the meaning of the
words "freely associated" in the Balfour declaration of 1926,
and to the discussion which continued up to World War II
on the question of whether the freedom of association included within its ambit freedom to withdraw. The answer to
this question was given with disarming simplicity by post-
1945 events: it is elementary Commonwealth constitutional
doctrine that a member may secede at will. Ireland seceded
in 1949; in 1961 South Africa did so by becoming a republic
and withdrawing her application for membership.

Who decides on admission to membership? This question
was raised in acute form by postwar developments and
particularly by the flood of applications for membership
starting with Ghana early in 1957. In 1951, the British House
of Commons was told that while the decision to grant independence was a matter exclusively between the United
Kingdom and the territory concerned, the question of
whether the territory should be admitted to the Common-

wealth was one for the existing membership of the association. When in 1956 the terms of Ghanaian independence were announced to the House of Commons, the Colonial Secretary made the same point and distinction. The case of Ghana was a critical one, for South Africa looked with grave doubt at the implications of African membership. But South Africa did not press her opposition, and the 1957 Conference of Commonwealth Prime Ministers welcomed Malaya and Ghana as members. Since then, each former colony or dependency, as it has become an independent state, has been accepted by the existing membership as a member of the Commonwealth.

We do not know what the association rules are—whether there must be a unanimous or a majority vote of the existing membership to bring in a new member—and it may be a fair assumption, so far anyway, that there are no rules. We know from the cases, and notably that of South Africa, that when a member changes its constitutional shape and converts to a republican status, it must renew its application for membership. Except in the case of South Africa, all Commonwealth countries converting to republican status have been readmitted.

The case of South Africa has already been briefly discussed, but it calls for fuller consideration. South Africa was not expelled from the Commonwealth; it withdrew its application. In a practical sense this is more appropriately treated as a case of secession. There had been talk of expulsion, for

South Africa's race policies were almost intolerably provocative to a multiracial Commonwealth. But it did not come to that, and we have no law or practice on expulsion from the Commonwealth. As Wheare points out,[18] the whole question of expulsion is obscure. Does expulsion mean that a member is excluded by unanimous vote of the existing members, excluding the expellee, or by a majority, or by a stipulated majority? Or does it mean that those members of the association who desire the expulsion of the offender themselves secede and form another association? Once again, the reality is likely to be that there is no jurisprudence of expulsion. All that is certain is that any initiative to expel a member or members would certainly produce acute divisions within the association.

The South African case has been explored in detail by Professor J. D. B. Miller, one of the foremost contemporary students of Commonwealth affairs, and the present account owes much to his work.[19] When the South African representative raised the question of continuing membership as a republic at the Prime Ministers' meeting in 1960, some sharp things were said about her racial policies. This was a time when the winds of change were blowing very hard in Africa, and the British Prime Minister had publicly expressed sympathetic understanding of African aspirations. By the time of the next meeting, in 1961, when South Africa's application came before the Prime Ministers, Nigeria, the African giant, had become a member of the Commonwealth, and it was reported that Julius Nyerere, the Tanganyikan nationalist leader, had said that his country, on attaining independence, would not seek membership if South Africa were still a member.

At the 1961 meeting, as the communiqué discloses, South African racial policies were discussed with the consent of South Africa. That was obviously a sharp and angry discussion, and the communiqué then narrates that

> . . . the Prime Minister of South Africa informed the other Prime Ministers this evening that in light of the views expressed on behalf of other member Governments and the indications of their future intentions regarding the racial policies of the Union Government, he had decided to withdraw his application for South Africa's continuing membership of the Commonwealth as a republic.

Miller suggests that the situation changed in the course of the debate. At first it was believed that a formula might be devised to preserve South Africa's membership, but at the end it appeared that only the Prime Ministers of Australia, New Zealand, and the Central African Federation supported the view that South Africa should stay. By way of explanation, the Central African Federation (now defunct) comprised the two Rhodesias and Nyasaland. It had been agreed that the Prime Minister of Southern Rhodesia, a self-governing colony since the early 1920's, should attend Commonwealth Prime Ministers' Conferences; thus when the

Central African Federation was established in 1953, its Prime Minister fell heir to the Southern Rhodesian seat. Sir Robert Menzies' position, supported by his small band of associates, was that a fundamental question was at stake: the principle of non-interference in the internal affairs of a member state. He had stated this principle in characteristic style in a speech at Cambridge University the previous year:

> We of the Commonwealth are no longer a single integrated structure, with a common foundation and a powerful organic association. Our strength is that we meet as equals, without vote or lobby; we speak to each other with freedom and friendliness; we seek to understand each other, but we do not sit in judgment on each other; we take an interest in each other but respect the fact that each member has achieved self-government; hence we seek to co-operate with each other but not to invade the sovereignty of each other.

At war in this case were two views of the Commonwealth. On the one side was the view expressed by Menzies that the Commonwealth is a historic and organic association to which entry is secured on attaining independence from a former status as a British dependency. The family traditions are, if anything, rather broad beliefs about government and law. But members do not sit in judgment on one another, and on matters of internal policy there is no call for, and no place for, a Commonwealth rule of decision. On the other side it was argued that there were limits to the principle of non-interference. The association does not sit in judgment on Pakistan for abandoning parliamentary institutions, nor on Ghana for what many regarded as departures from accepted democratic standards. But in the multiracial Commonwealth, a member state like South Africa which rejects racial equality denies the fundamental principle on which the Commonwealth is now based. As Mr. Duncan Sandys, the British Secretary of State for Commonwealth Affairs said, "It must . . . be recognized that apartheid has aroused deep emotions throughout the world and has ceased to be a matter of purely domestic concern." [20] Of this there can be no doubt.

It has been said that some of the older members of the Commonwealth felt a sense of failure over the South African withdrawal and that this is reflected in a rather more strained and uncomfortable view of the association. This may be so; it is still too early to tell, but it draws attention to the difficulties which arise within a multiracial Commonwealth. It may be that the departure of South Africa will ease the effort of living within the multiracial Commonwealth, for there is no other state within the association which poses comparable problems or strains. A question has been raised, following these events, whether the rules of the association are now changed so that the internal policies of member states are open to discussion, criticism, and maybe cesure at Commonwealth meetings.

To this the formal answer may be given that South Africa expressly agreed to allow discussion of her racial policies by the Prime Ministers in 1961, and the substantive answer that this particular case, so provocative to the multiracial Commonwealth, was special. Miller's judgment, at this point of time, seems to me to be right.[21]

> South Africa . . . can justifiably be regarded as an exception to the normal course of Commonwealth affairs which includes agreement to differ and mutual tolerance of one nation's behavior by another. It is not to be expected that any radical change will occur in either the structure or the characteristic mode of action of the Commonwealth as a result of South Africa's departure.

III

With the disappearance of institutional links in the Commonwealth, the emphasis has shifted, not surprisingly, to a study of the *motion* of the association. The 1926 Conference, in its report, said of the Commonwealth that "free cooperation is its instrument," and many of the stresses in contemporary discussion are on consultation and cooperation between Commonwealth members. A decade ago, a former Secretary of State for Commonwealth Relations wrote that

... although there are no treaty commitments and no permanent machinery for evolving common policies, there is one thing that helps us to keep near to each other, and that is the habit which has now become ingrained, of consultation. Consultation between the Commonwealth countries is much more constant, friendly and comprehensive than would be usual or even possible, between foreign States, even though they were the closest allies. Each member of the Commonwealth recognizes its duty to consult and its right to be consulted. This is a continuing process, and not just brought into use at a time of crisis, and this constant "give and take" has the gradual effect of narrowing down differences that may exist between us, or at least enabling differences to be understood.[22]

Sir Robert Menzies propounded the rule of consultation in 1956. "I am no carping critic; but I would courteously suggest that one text might be boldly printed in every department in London, New Delhi, Canberra and the other Seats of Government. Will any decision I am today contemplating affect some other nation of the Commonwealth?" That was an unfortunate year to phrase the question in such a way, for it was the year of Suez, the *annus horribilis* of non-consultation. But of that, more hereafter.

In 1916, in the middle of World War I, the British Prime Minister, Lloyd George, wrote:

I am convinced that we should take the Dominions into our counsels in much larger measure. . . . As we must receive even more substantial support from them before we can pull through, it is important that they should be made to feel that they have a share in our counsels as well as in our burdens.

So in 1917 the Imperial War Cabinet came into existence and dominion political leaders sat with members of the United Kingdom government discharging the responsibility for directing the war effort. But in the normal constitutional sense it was not a cabinet. It was not collectively responsible to anyone; it was rather a standing conference of a group of nations engaged in a great common war enterprise. It broke up in 1919, and during the inter-war years the somewhat formal and cumbrous Imperial Conference served as the principal machinery for Commonwealth consultation. On the outbreak of war in 1939 there was a proposal to revive the Imperial War Cabinet, but it was the view of most Commonwealth political leaders that communication and cooperation between their governments were better secured by greater informality and that the international telephone and airplane made speedy communication a relatively simple matter.

Subsequent proposals to provide more formal machinery for Commonwealth consultation have had little success. In 1943 the Australian Prime Minister, Mr. Curtin, proposed the creation of a Commonwealth Secretariat which, as a permanent organization, would give more practical and coherent expression to the association's purposes and activities. This proposal was not acceptable to Canada, South Africa, or New Zealand. In 1948 it was revived by Lord Bruce, a former Australian Prime Minister who had had considerable experience of Commonwealth affairs. He proposed a permanent consultative council. Again the response was unfavorable. As Field Marshal Smuts put it, "the more machinery we have, the more friction there will be." Australia continued to carry the torch, and in 1957 Sir Robert Menzies renewed the proposal for the establishment of a consultative council. The proposal was modest and cautious, and while the response was less unfavorable, nothing has come of it. Recent events make it less likely that complex organizational machinery will be devised, though as membership grows— and it has grown very considerably since 1957—the organizational problems of the association become much greater.

Since the end of World War II, the formal Imperial Conferences have given place to the less formal meetings of Commonwealth Prime Ministers, the first of which was held in London in 1944. Those who have participated in such meetings have spoken warmly of them as furnishing a means by which leaders may reach a meeting of minds on matters of common concern. Such matters, as the communiqués reveal (so far as they reveal), transcend purely intra-Commonwealth affairs, and indeed much of the discussion has been on the great international issues of the day, though the most recent meetings have been concerned with great

Commonwealth themes: South African membership and racialism, and the Common Market and the Commonwealth. Lord Attlee, who as British Prime Minister presided over the early postwar meetings, has described their procedure: the intent was to arrive at a consensus without a formal vote, and there was a rule of non-discussion of matters of intra-Commonwealth dispute which was meticulously observed at the formal meetings. He instances the case of Kashmir which, he says, was never discussed by the Prime Ministers at the formal conference table, though outside the conference room there were frequent endeavors by him and by other Prime Ministers to devise a solution acceptable to India and Pakistan.

The Prime Ministers' meetings are the consultative summit; and below the summit, consultation and cooperation go on, formally and informally, at many levels. There are meetings of Commonwealth economic and foreign ministers held from time to time at various places in the Commonwealth. The Colombo Plan had its genesis in such a meeting of foreign ministers held at Colombo in 1950. There have been conferences of Commonwealth representatives on various matters more or less specialized; these include education (involving scholarships and exchanges of students and scholars between Commonwealth countries), science, nuclear science, telecommunications, social insurance, agricultural bureaus, and nationality and citizenship. There are regular conferences on such matters as forestry, the press and broadcasting, and periodical meetings of specialists like survey officers and auditors-general. There are bureaus, offices, boards, committees, associations, institutes, and commissions, with headquarters for the most part in London, which deal with specialist matters. Lord Attlee records that at the United Nations Charter Conference held at San Francisco in 1945, he presided over regular morning meetings of the Commonwealth delegates. Lord Franks has told of the regular fortnightly meetings of Commonwealth Ambassadors in Washington. "The discussions," he writes, "took place between like-minded people who shared a common political tradition. No one had to insist on the freedom of his country because nobody ever questioned it. We had forbearance which is essential between members of a continuing club." [23]

The Commonwealth Relations Office in the United Kingdom plays an especially important role in Commonwealth consultation and cooperation. The Office has an ancestry going back to Colonial days. A special dominions division of the Colonial Office was set up in 1907, and in 1925 a separate Dominions Office was created because the existing organization was "inadequate to the extent and variety of the work thrown upon it." For a time the offices of Secretary for the Colonies and Secretary for the Dominions were held in one pair of hands; then they were separated; and recently, as Britain's colonial commitments have dwindled, the two offices have again been held by one Minister. The Dominions

Office absorbed the India Office when it lost its *raison d'être* with Indian independence in 1947, and the name of the office was changed in that year to the Commonwealth Relations Office. No other Commonwealth country has a separate office or department which concerns itself exclusively with Commonwealth affairs; the United Kingdom Office and its principal officer, the Secretary of State, are tangible evidence of the fact that the Commonwealth has been *au fond* a pre-eminent concern of the mother country. The Secretary of State speaks in the United Kingdom government with a distinctively Commonwealth voice, and the Office is a great clearinghouse of information for the Commonwealth as a whole on matters which concern its various members. These activities have been described by an English spokesman for the Office:

> We pump out an extraordinary quantity of information to the various Commonwealth countries. We try to keep them in touch with foreign affairs and economic affairs and defense matters and even things like atomic energy. . . . Naturally this varies a great deal. Canada may not be interested in something which is of interest to a South Asian country; South Africa may not be interested in various things of interest to Pakistan, and so on. Our object is to give the fullest information we can. It may not always be possible to give immediate information. A situation has got to reach a certain point before you can say something about it, and everyone has his own responsibility for making his own decision.[24]

6 7

The regular functions of representation, normally discharged by Ambassadors, are, as between Commonwealth countries, performed by High Commissioners. The formulation of the status of the Governor-General in the 1920's as a personal representative of the Crown meant that he ceased to be a spokesman for or representative of the United Kingdom government. So it happened that United Kingdom government representatives were appointed to the various Commonwealth countries, starting in 1928 with Canada. The United Kingdom has High Commissioners in all Commonwealth countries, and they, reciprocally, all have High Commissioners in the United Kingdom. As between other Commonwealth countries, there is also an exchange of High Commissioners, save that in particular cases appointments are not made because the work and expense do not warrant it. The High Commissioners have ambassadorial status and privileges, though in certain respects they operate rather differently. The differences lie in the machinery of communication and dealing. As described by a senior officer of the Commonwealth Relations Office:

Whereas [an] Ambassador must do all his business through the Department of External Affairs, the High Commissioner is entitled to deal direct with other departments of government. The result is that the High Commissioner and his staff at appropriate levels have contacts of an informal sort through the machinery of Government. A point of particular note is that the United Kingdom High Commissioner has closer and more frequent contact with the Prime Minister of the Commonwealth country in which he is serving than is the case with foreign heads of missions. Practice on this point naturally varies, but in Australia, for instance, on all important matters and whenever a formal approach is called for, the High Commissioner deals direct with the Prime Minister.[25]

All of this is a description of machinery, and the machinery is impressive. As to some parts, at least, of this machinery, it has to be recognized, as the *London Economist* observed in its comment on the Prime Ministers' Conference on the Common Market in September 1962, that as the Commonwealth becomes fragmented into more and more states, discussion inevitably gets more rambling, less purposeful, and more demagogic, and that Commonwealth meetings may come to look more like United Nations meetings.[26] As Wheare has well said,

It is clear that in a world-wide Commonwealth with members whose vital interests are affected by different forces in different parts of the world and whose policies consequently are extremely difficult to harmonize, cooperation must be expected to be difficult and to get more difficult before it gets easier.[27]

If, one may add, it ever gets easier. The fact is that on important issues and questions Commonwealth countries take very different and sometimes mutually hostile positions.

We know of the divisions between India and Pakistan. We know that there are sharp differences on foreign policy within the Commonwealth which we shall have to explore later in greater detail. The relations of some Commonwealth countries are more intimate and comfortable with countries outside the association than with countries inside it. As we are well reminded, all roads in the Commonwealth lead to Washington,[28] though, if the metaphor may be extended, only some of the roads are super-highways.

In 1946 Mr. Attlee, then Prime Minister of the United Kingdom, said in the House of Commons that

> It is our practice and our duty as members of the British Commonwealth, to keep other members of the Commonwealth fully and continuously informed of all matters which we are called upon to decide, but which may affect Commonwealth interests. The object is to give them an opportunity of expressing their views in confidence, if they so desire. These views are taken fully into account, but the decision must be ours, and the other Governments are not asked, and would not wish, to share the responsibility for it. Dominion Governments follow the same practice.

In 1946 the association had not yet diversified into the multiracial Commonwealth, but since that time, and notwithstanding the great changes that have occurred, Commonwealth leaders have asserted and reasserted the duty to consult and the right to be consulted on matters which affect the interests of the association and its members.

But it is clear that there are very real limits to the extent and efficacy of consultation and cooperation between Commonwealth members who view the world very differently and whose judgments and evaluations lead them to take differing positions on matters of defense and foreign policy. While at technical levels there may be defense cooperation among members on such matters as military equipment, staff and officer training, and so on, it is not likely that this will carry over into defense policy in those areas in which members of the Commonwealth pursue differing and, it may be, antagonistic policies. Indeed, it is more appropriate to say that at the present day

> . . . members of the Commonwealth habitually inform one another of their policies, unless they consider that they will be inconvenienced by doing so. . . . At the same time they may consider that their own long-term national interest in the preservation of the Commonwealth outweighs some short-term national interest. Consultation means information, when and how the informer pleases.[29]

This estimate of contemporary performance was formulated in light of the Suez events at the end of 1956. The British action against Egypt had profoundly divisive effects within the Commonwealth; only Australia and New Zealand lent clear support to the United Kingdom, and even within those countries there were sharp divisions over the issues. To Asian and African members, the British action was seen as a reversion to "gunboat" diplomacy, recalling the high noon of colonialism, and as such it was intolerable. India played a conspicuous role in the attack on the United Kingdom in the United Nations, and she had strong support from other Asian and African Commonwealth countries. To Canada, with her deep concern for maintaining harmonious links with the Commonwealth (and within it) and with the United States, the British action came as a profound shock.

The fact was, of course, that the British action at Suez was undertaken without any consultation at all with the Commonwealth. The British Prime Minister, Sir Anthony Eden, defended his government's action on the ground that consultation was impossible because of the time factor; action had to be taken immediately, if at all. A more elaborate argument in support of the British action joined with the time factor the consideration that no measure of consultation would have gained the agreement of the African and Asian members of the Commonwealth, or of Canada, so that consultation was pointless. Consultation was one thing; restricting Britain to a course of action acceptable to all members of the Commonwealth was quite another.

The Canadian judgment was expressed by Mr. Lester Pearson, then Minister for External Affairs. He said that during the crisis the Commonwealth was "badly and dangerously split," that it was "on the verge of dissolution," and that Canada was not "a colonial chore-boy running around shouting 'ready, aye, ready.' " [30] Canadian opinion was not unanimous; there was present a measure of support for the mother country. Nor was Australian opinion unanimous; although Sir Robert Menzies, a most eloquent advocate of consultation, with equal eloquence supported British action in Suez, there was doubt within the ranks of his own party and strong opposition outside it.

One may guess that Suez was a "once-only" episode; its very failure in execution, its success in uniting all manner of unlikely forces in opposition to it, and its profoundly divisive effects on the Commonwealth cumulatively make it very unlikely that comparable action would ever be taken again.

But the fact that the heart country of the Commonwealth undertook this solitary action at Suez threw a strong light on the character of the consultation requirement of membership of the association. The action could not be squared with the principles enunciated by the Imperial Conference of 1926, nor with those stated by Mr. Attlee in 1946, nor with those principles, going forward into the era of the multi-racial Commonwealth, propounded by Lord Ismay, a former Secretary of State for Commonwealth Relations, that "each member of the Commonwealth recognizes its duty to consult and its right to be consulted." No one would be so inane as to suggest that the United Kingdom forgot or overlooked the rule. The action was taken because it represented a judgment of important British interests which could not be secured without rapid and secret action, and which could never be expected to command the support of many members of the Commonwealth. It may be that the British government reckoned on speedy success and the presentation of a *fait accompli* which could withstand the buffetings of angry critics in debate. But putting such speculation aside, British action at Suez, translated into Commonwealth doctrine, surely means what Miller says it means: that what will ultimately prevail will be the interest of the member state, and it by no means follows that there will invariably be consultation. And while there is, and continues to be, a significant measure of consultation and cooperation, the old categorical rules of consultation cannot make sense in sensitive areas of policy where Commonwealth views and interests reflect division and diversities which extend far beyond the limits of the Commonwealth.

III

The Politics
and Prospects
of the Contemporary
Commonwealth

THE TWO WORLD WARS worked profound changes in the character of the Commonwealth. The first accelerated the motion of constitutional and institutional change; the second was the catalyst of the multiracial Commonwealth. The Second World War also projected the member states of the Commonwealth onto the world stage. Foreign policy, it has been said, became the principal preoccupation of the members of the Commonwealth after 1945.[1]

The member states of the pre-1914 Commonwealth were not equipped to deal as independent states with issues of foreign affairs. Neither the Canadian Constitution, which was enacted in 1867, nor the Australian Constitution of 1900 contained treaty-making powers, and this was not oversight. External affairs were for Whitehall and not for Ottawa or

Canberra. An Australian constitutionalist, writing a few years before the First World War, said that "it is no part of the executive power of the Commonwealth to make treaties with foreign powers," [2] and as late as 1923 three judges of the Australian High Court, in the course of a joint opinion, found it "difficult to imagine an Ambassador to Australia." [3] All three judges survived to see that difficulty disappear in the post-1945 period. Nor did it prove to be beyond judicial capacity to discover in the Canadian and Australian constitutions sources of authority for the exercise of treaty-making powers when changing circumstances called for them, though, notably in the case of Canada, difficulties arose in the context of treaty implementation. I have told that story elsewhere. [4] There is a striking difference in this respect between these older Commonwealth constitutions and those of the post-1945 Commonwealth members, which were born as independent countries, fully and consciously endowed with the constitutional apparatus for the conduct of international affairs and independent foreign policies.

The events of the First World War moved the older Commonwealth countries to demand some voice in the shaping of imperial foreign policies. Sir Robert Borden of Canada claimed for them in 1917 "an adequate voice in foreign policy in future." They were assigned separate representation at the Paris Peace Conference and signed the peace treaties separately, though they retained membership of the British Empire delegation and appended their signatures to the treaties under the heading of the British Empire. Australia, New Zealand, and South Africa became mandatories under the League of Nations. And in the early 1920's Canada and South Africa made it clear that they would not follow unquestioningly a British foreign policy in the making of which they had no part. They told the United Kingdom government, which had gone to the verge of war with Turkey at Chanak in 1923, that any decision to send help must lie with their legislatures. In 1923 an Imperial Conference affirmed an independent treaty-making power in the dominions, and Canada blazed a trail by negotiating and signing in her own right a treaty with the United States for the regulation of halibut fishing on the Pacific Coast. When the United Kingdom became a party to the Locarno Treaty in 1925, it was expressly declared that the dominions and India should not be parties to its provisions unless they gave their assent, and that assent was not forthcoming. In 1926 the Imperial Conference declared that the principles of autonomy and equality in Commonwealth relations extended to the conduct of foreign affairs.

Despite these developments, Commonwealth countries took few and very uncertain steps on the international stage during the inter-war years. Their resources and expertise were small, and they showed little inclination to take independent initiatives in international politics. So far as the relations of Commonwealth countries *inter se* were concerned, the view was still expressed that, unlike the relations of foreign states, they were not truly international.[5] Talk of joint control of an imperial foreign policy, which gathered strength in the latter days of the First World War, proved to be nothing more than talk, for it lacked reality and practicality. There were few independent initiatives taken by the dominions in foreign policy in these years; rather they operated as brakes and restraints upon British action, and until the fall of Prague early in 1939, appeasement was a general Commonwealth policy.[6]

The Second World War worked a profound change. The events which occurred at its outbreak made it clear, as we have seen, that decisions as to peace and war are for the individual members of the Commonwealth. The crushing blows of the first year, followed by the entry of Japan into the war at the end of 1941, exposed very starkly the incapacity of the United Kingdom to furnish protection for the Commonwealth. There were sharp differences between the Australian and United Kingdom Prime Ministers over the use of Australian troops in face of the Japanese threat to Australia in 1942. Australia and New Zealand demanded a Pacific War Council in Washington in 1942 so that their views on the conduct of the war could be represented directly to the American government and not indirectly through United Kingdom spokesmen.

The decline in United Kingdom power and the perception of the fact that the principal British strategic and defense interests lay in Europe also prompted a reformulation of Commonwealth responsibilities. This was developed by Dr. Evatt as Australian Minister for External Affairs in 1946: [7]

> It is sufficient to suggest that an entirely new concept in British Commonwealth relations is now emerging [which] involves the possibility of a Dominion acting in certain regions or for certain purposes on behalf of the other members of the British Commonwealth including the United Kingdom itself. There is evidence that the machinery of cooperation between nations of the British Commonwealth has now reached a stage where a common policy can be carried out through a chosen Dominion instrumentality in an area or in relation to a subject matter which is of primary concern to that Dominion. This principle is capable of extension and suggests the possible integration of British Commonwealth policy at a higher level by a new procedure. Its importance is very great and may rapidly increase.

In 1944 Australia and New Zealand concluded a pact which was primarily concerned with defense, but also contemplated cooperation in other fields, particularly in the promotion of the welfare of the native peoples of the Pacific. In the postwar period an Australian was appointed as Commander-in-Chief of the British Commonwealth occupation force in Japan, and there were single Commonwealth representatives on the Japanese War Crimes Commission and on the Advisory Council in Tokyo during the allied occupation of

Japan. It was on an Australian motion that an informal Commonwealth conference met at Canberra in 1947 to discuss the terms of the Japanese Peace Treaty, and the formulation of the Colombo Plan in 1950 owed much to Australian initiative at a Commonwealth foreign ministers' meeting.

But the possibility of extensive action along these lines is limited, for postwar developments show, clearly enough, that there is not a distinctive Commonwealth policy on most important issues of international politics. From the date of the San Francisco Conference on the United Nations Charter, up to the present day, it has been clear that issues of international policy and organization actually divide members of the Commonwealth. At San Francisco, the United Kingdom was ranged on one side and Australia, New Zealand, and, with some qualifications, Canada, on the other over the issue of Great Power domination of the United Nations. As Mr. McKenzie King put it, "we were fighting to prevent two countries from dominating the world, and we do not now wish to see any one, two, three or four countries dominate the peace." The battle that was lost over the veto was carried into other areas of the Charter, and there the success was greater.

All member states of the Commonwealth are members of the United Nations. Ceylon was for a time the victim of the membership deadlock which was resolved in the mid-1950's, and since that time each Commonwealth country on attain-

ing independence has become a member. Study of the performance and votes of Commonwealth countries in the
United Nations shows that they do not in any sense con-
stitute a voting *bloc*, and that, on the contrary, many issues
tend to divide them. Such matters as the seating of Communist China in the United Nations; the conduct of the
Korean War; the Suez crisis; until comparatively recently,
the apartheid policies of South Africa; and more recently,
virtually all issues touching colonialism, including trustee-
ship, have found Commonwealth countries in different
camps, sometimes very bitterly divided. Positions have not
always been maintained without shift, but the divisions are
often sharp. What indeed has been specially significant in
this regard has been the introduction of intra-Commonwealth disputes into the United Nations arena. The
Imperial Conferences of 1926–1930 envisaged the creation of
machinery for the resolution of such disputes so that dirty
Commonwealth linen should not be washed on the world
stage, but this never materialized. The two major intra-
Commonwealth disputes aired in the United Nations have
been the Indian-Pakistani controversy over Kashmir which
was brought before the Security Council, and the complaint
by India against South Africa over the treatment of Indians
in that country which was first raised in the General Assembly in 1946. In neither case was an objection to compe-
tence raised on the ground that this was a familial, intra-

Commonwealth issue; South Africa's objection to the Indian complaint was that the matter was one of domestic jurisdiction under Section 2(7) of the Charter.

The record of Commonwealth performance in the United Nations has been summarized in a recent study:

> We may say, first, that while extensive and continual consultation is an effective link between all Commonwealth countries, they do not form a consistent bloc or group and that they are more often in United Nations action divided than united; secondly that the principle of which the United Kingdom has been the special custodian that the relations between Commonwealth countries are not foreign relations, but are in a sense private and familial, is now submerged in the wider sense of obligation which Commonwealth countries now feel primarily to the United Nations, of which they are all members; and lastly, that the increased membership of the United Nations, particularly of African and Asian countries, will tend to intensify the divisions between the older and newer members of the Commonwealth in United Nations debates and actions.[8]

There follows an expression of hope that the objective of a multiracial Commonwealth, if it is attained, may counter these fissiparous tendencies and make the Commonwealth a force within the United Nations. But this is not present reality and, as I read the situation, there is little evidence at this time that it is likely to be achieved.

The divisions between Commonwealth countries within

the United Nations are a reflection of broader divisions on the world stage. To the older members of the Commonwealth, the rise of Soviet and Communist power generally have posed major problems of defense and security. To India in particular, and to a substantial body of Afro-Asian Commonwealth opinion, bloc attitudes and dispositions have not been acceptable. The differences of viewpoint were well phrased by the *rapporteur* of the discussions at the Commonwealth Conference at Lahore, Pakistan, in 1954:

The representatives of the older members of the Commonwealth, for some time accustomed to the pains as well as to the satisfactions of sovereignty, presumed that the world remained what in their experience it had long been, a place of danger. . . . In their preoccupation with security . . . they displayed what seemed to some of their Asian colleagues an almost shocking fluency in speaking of the indispensability of horrible weapons of war to preserve peace. . . . But for the Asian members . . . their experience of sovereignty in the modern world had been briefer and, during the critical years of Communist expansion in Europe, very different. With memories overshadowed by past conflicts with imperial Powers, they regarded the post-war struggle between the Communist and non-Communist world not indeed with indifference but somewhat remotely.[9]

Recent Indian experience with China has surely affected her thinking on issues of security but has not produced a dramatic change in her approach to major issues of foreign policy. However, to a Commonwealth country in the position of Canada, security considerations have loomed large and to her the establishment of an association like NATO was an act of fundamental importance. In face of a perceived and urgent threat of Soviet aggression against Western Europe, and in face of a Security Council politically paralyzed by the Cold War and incapable of furnishing security in Western Europe, NATO was an appropriate, indeed *the* appropriate, response. And for Canada it had the special merit of bringing into close alliance the United States, the United Kingdom, and Western Europe. As Mr. Lester Pearson put it:

> For us NATO is especially significant, as it reconciles the forces of geography and history in our national political evolution. In doing so it helps to dissipate the nightmare that used to frighten every Canadian government; a serious divergence in policy between neighbor and mother country.

India's reaction to NATO was at first noncommittal, but it hardened as she became increasingly discontented with Western policy and as NATO came to be seen in Indian eyes as a protector of the colonial possessions of its European members—a reading which India's fellow members of the Commonwealth within NATO would surely have repudiated. But bitter Indian criticism was reserved for SEATO, which included in its membership the United Kingdom, Australia, New Zealand, and Pakistan. SEATO was seen by its architects in 1954 as an alliance to shore up non-Communist Southeast Asia in face of an urgent and dangerous Communist threat to the area in the aftermath of the Indo-Chinese debacle. To Mr. Nehru, it was a non-Asian intrusion into Asia, an extension of bloc politics into an area which wanted to be free of them. It was this aspect of SEATO which India most strongly resented, and Pakistani membership in the pact also provoked an Indian charge that its members favored Pakistan in its dispute with India over Kashmir. Australia, in adhering to the SEATO pact, expressly stated that this did not commit her to any position in the Kashmir dispute. The Indian criticism of SEATO was also leveled at the alliance once known as the Baghdad Pact and later as CENTO, of which two members of the Commonwealth, the United Kingdom and Pakistan, were members.

From this very brief account of post-1945 history, it is apparent that Commonwealth countries find themselves in opposition to one another on issues of international politics, sometimes in very sharp opposition. India's attack on Commonwealth participation in SEATO is a notable example, and her attack on the United Kingdom for its part in the Suez events of 1956 was vehement and unrelenting. But the divisions within the Commonwealth on issues of international politics are complex; it is gross oversimplification to describe them wholly as disputes between old and new, purely in terms of division between racial and cultural blocs. For there are also difficult and persistent issues which divide India and Pakistan, recurring disputes between India and Ceylon, and divisions within independent Africa which find Commonwealth members ranged on opposing sides.

There is, too, the important consideration that postwar alliances have brought Commonwealth members into alliance with non-Commonwealth members. This is true of the various regional groupings to which I have referred. The emergence of the United States as the leader of the free world has made her a focal point in many of the alliances and associations. To repeat an apt phrase, all roads in the Commonwealth now lead to Washington, and an Indian observer has suggested that "the ultimate, though not the intended effect of the United States diplomacy may be to promote the security of the individual members of the Commonwealth at the expense of the unity of the Commonwealth as a whole." [10] Such was the reading, by some anyway, of the ANZUS Pact of 1951 in which Australia, New Zealand, and the United States joined at the time of the conclusion of the Japanese Peace Treaty. This was the first treaty signed by Australia and New Zealand with a foreign country; it made clear the military dependence of these two Commonwealth members on the United States, and the United Kingdom was specifically excluded from its operation. This exclusion was much disliked by Sir Winston Churchill, who shortly afterwards became Prime Minister of the United Kingdom, and there were critics in Australia and New Zealand who charged their governments with unfilial conduct in not insisting on a place in the alliance for the United Kingdom. The reason for United Kingdom exclusion has been debated,[11] but it was pointed out, and properly, that the pact should not be read as an unfilial act or as a rejection of the mother country; it acknowledged and asserted the plain and obvious fact that the security and defense of the Antipodean members of the Commonwealth depended upon the support of the United States.

A Pakistani Prime Minister observed early in the postwar period that "an independent foreign policy and membership of the Commonwealth are not necessarily mutually opposed things." That is certainly true; history since 1945 affords abundant testimony. The defense and foreign policies of individual Commonwealth countries may bind them much more closely to non-Commonwealth countries, notably the United States, than to fellow members of the Commonwealth, whose wave lengths may also be harder to reach. It seems almost trite to say that the Commonwealth is not—and as far forward as I can see, will not be—a coherent, cohesive, and identifiable grouping in foreign relations and international politics. I find inexplicable the comment of a Canadian writer in 1956 that "in times of danger they [the members of the Commonwealth] work together like a well drilled team." [12] Unless I misunderstand its thrust, it was not true in

1956 (the year of Suez); it is not now true in a more highly diversified Commonwealth with a substantial, and certainly not united, African component in its membership; and it is not likely to be true in the future. One may say, perhaps, that patterns and habits of consultation serve, at least on occasion, to moderate divisions and differences between members of the Commonwealth and that the availability of intra-Commonwealth channels of communication affords easier and fuller understanding of differing points of view. But too much should not be made of this, and I think its significance is diminishing in the association as a whole.

II

What of economic ties? Much was heard of these during the Common Market debates of 1961–1962. As British interest in the European Economic Community grew, the concern of Commonwealth countries with the impact of United Kingdom membership of the Community on their economies likewise increased. In July 1961 four senior United Kingdom ministers visited Commonwealth capitals to consult with the governments on the question of the United Kingdom's relations with the European Economic Community. The first "full dress" Commonwealth discussion of the situation took place at the meeting of Commonwealth Finance Ministers at Accra, Ghana, in September 1961. The United Kingdom stated the reasons which led it to take a Community course. Representatives of Commonwealth countries expressed their fears and stressed the value and importance they attached to established Commonwealth trading arrangements. To this the United Kingdom delegation replied that until the market negotiations developed it was not possible to ascertain whether satisfactory arrangements could be made to safeguard the economic interests of Commonwealth countries, but that there would be continuing and close negotiations with all Commonwealth governments at all stages of the negotiations. In London, in the same month, Mr. Sandys, the Secretary of State for Commonwealth Affairs, told the Commonwealth Parliamentary Conference that "if the negotiations fail and we are unable to secure special arrangements to protect vital Commonwealth interests, then Britain will not join the Common Market. That is our declared position and we have no intention of shifting from it."

During 1962 spokesmen for various Commonwealth countries elaborated on the injury that would be suffered by them individually, and the damage that would be done to the structure of the Commonwealth as a whole, if the United Kingdom entered the Community without appropriate safeguards and guaranties for Commonwealth interests. These interests were threatened in two ways: first, by the loss of imperial preferences, which gave Commonwealth products a preferred positions over non-Commonwealth products in the United Kingdom market; second, by the extension of the common external tariff wall of the Community to the United Kingdom. The extension of the tariff wall would afford a preference over Commonwealth products to the competing products of Community countries.

The 1962 debate over United Kingdom entry into the Community was not a simple issue between the United Kingdom on the one side and Commonwealth members on the other. Within the United Kingdom itself there was a sharp debate, phrased in economic, political, historical, and also in sentimental terms, on the wisdom and propriety of the decision to join the Community, and there was much concern over the impact on the Commonwealth of British entry. It seems clear—and this emerges from the communiqué of the Prime Ministers' Conference in September 1962—that the attitude of the United Kingdom government hardened in favor of British entry into the Community on the best obtainable terms for the Commonwealth. "We are independent, too," the United Kingdom Prime Minister reminded his unhappy Commonwealth colleagues.

While there are consultative institutions for Commonwealth trade, finance, and economic development—the Montreal Conference of Commonwealth Finance Ministers in 1958 resolved on the establishment of a comprehensive Commonwealth Economic Consultative Council—there are no general Commonwealth institutions in the trading field.

The system of Commonwealth or Imperial Preferences is generally dated back to the Ottawa Agreements of 1932, although there had previously been some similar arrangements made by individual Commonwealth countries. Under the Ottawa system the countries of the Commonwealth grant each other various tariff concessions with the object of increasing the flow of intra-Commonwealth trade. Apart from these Ottawa preferences, Commonwealth countries have granted various "non-contractual" preferences to each other in the normal structure of their tariffs. But the Ottawa agreements were bilateral; that is to say, they were worked out between individual Commonwealth members *inter se* with reference to particular aspects of their trade, and they had no provision for policy-making bodies for the preference system as a whole. Since 1945, some of these Commonwealth trading agreements have been reviewed to bring them up to date and into better balance. The effect has been to reduce the scope of the concessions, and other changes have been made in the course of the multilateral tariff negotiations carried out under the General Agreement on Tariffs and Trade.

During the Common Market debate, these imperial preferences certainly assumed large importance. Yet there is no doubt that their value had declined with rising prices in recent years. And they did not cover the major exports of a number of Commonwealth countries, including wool, wheat, metals, and jute. The export of some, though not all, of these commodities to the United Kingdom would have been prejudicially affected by the extension of the Common Market external tariff wall. For the United Kingdom, imperial preference had given an advantage to British-manufactured goods in Commonwealth markets over the products of non-Commonwealth manufacturers. But within the Commonwealth British manufacturers, struggling to expand markets, were faced with serious problems. They had to meet formidable competition from *local* favored manufactures which no Commonwealth country was willing to discourage, and which, indeed, were encouraged and stimulated. Also, in face of recurrent balance-of-payments problems, some Commonwealth countries imposed import restrictions. Australia did this on occasion during the 1950's, which had an adverse impact on United Kingdom trade and drew protests from United Kingdom exporting interests.

The structure of imperial preferences never succeeded in constructing a "closed" system of trading within the Commonwealth. The diversification and industrialization of individual Commonwealth economies have worked against this, and British governments have been attracted by the availability of cheap food imports from outside the Commonwealth. Of growing importance too has been the fact that expanding markets for Commonwealth products have opened up outside the Commonwealth, as evidenced by the growth of Australian trade with Asia and notably with Japan. Such trading patterns obviously work against the extension of a Commonwealth preferential trading system, for such an extension would prejudice the maintenance and growth of these important and growing trade relationships between Commonwealth and non-Commonwealth countries.

Such developments have not encouraged the growth and extension of imperial preferences, though these preferences still afford opportunities and advantages to certain Commonwealth industries in United Kingdom markets, and there has been an understandable desire to preserve these advantages. But on the eve of the Common Market debate their significance as a bond of Commonwealth was not to be overstated. While a United Kingdom government publication in 1961 spoke of the preference structure as "a tangible and important link between the countries of the Commonwealth," [13] an independent estimate a few years earlier evaluated the system as

> peripherally advantageous, but in no sense comprehensive. While Commonwealth nations consider that they derive solid benefits from [imperial preference], these benefits are not enough in themselves to explain membership of the Commonwealth, and not enough to make the members resist attractive offers of trade from countries outside the Commonwealth such as Japan and Germany.[14]

And, it may be added, no Commonwealth country committed to a program of industrialization and economic diversification would be deflected from its course because of an adverse impact on the United Kingdom economy.

The United Kingdom decision to apply for entry into the European Economic Community appears to have been based on complex considerations. The British economy had been relatively stagnant, while the economies of the Community countries were growing vigorously, and it was believed that British industry would be rejuvenated and boosted by entry into the Community. There was the consideration that both the Community and the United Kingdom would be stronger with Britain as a member, and this was reinforced by strong American advocacy of British membership on political, economic, and defense grounds. So far as the Commonwealth was concerned, the facts disclosed a relative decline in the importance of trade between the United Kingdom and Commonwealth countries. And in relation to the Commonwealth, there was the general factor which Lord Casey has described as "its comparative inadequacy for political economic or defensive growth." [15]

Of course there were arguments which went the other way, and there were risks and uncertainties in a British commitment to the Community. But the government's decision, when it became firm, was strongly in favor of membership. And when the prospect (or threat) of British application for membership became an immediate reality, the Commonwealth response was immediate, urgent, and loud. The air was filled with jeremiads, of portents of economic losses of massive proportions. The potential losses and economic dislocation to the economies of individual Commonwealth countries were of differing orders of magnitude, and were, in some cases anyway, conjectural. A country like New Zealand, because of special trading relationships with the United Kingdom, faced special problems. It may well be that the United Kingdom government did not help itself by its changes of tune. It had earlier spoken of Commonwealth commitments and concerns as a major reason for standing apart from the Community; as late as the last quarter of 1961 government spokesmen had asserted a "declared position" that British entry into the Community was conditional on securing "special arrangements to protect vital Commonwealth interests." A year later the government's position was that the United Kingdom negotiators would do their best for the Commonwealth, but enter the Community Britain must.

The long-range economic and political impact on the interests of the Commonwealth of British Community membership, should it yet come about, is still uncertain. But this account surely supports the view of Lord Casey, a long-time practitioner of Commonwealth politics, that

> as things are at present each independent country of the Commonwealth has to act solely in the interests of its own people. No government can afford to be generous to other countries, even Commonwealth countries, or even afford to be *thought* generous. It is just hard bargaining with the cards held close to the chests of the bargainers. This elimi-

nates trade as a cohesive factor in the Commonwealth, except where the interests of two or more Commonwealth countries happen to coincide.[16]

Certainly no one reading the 1962 record of Commonwealth discussions can come away with any impression other than that the cloth of Commonwealth was exposed as pretty threadbare. I suspect that in the aftermath of the British failure to secure terms for entry into the Community there was some disenchantment with the Commonwealth in British hearts and minds, and it may also be that some Commonwealth leaders felt some discomfort in perhaps having shouted and pressed too hard and thereby contributed to the British humiliation. But in Commonwealth capitals there was relief that the economic problems were not so immediate and that there was more time to effect adjustments and insurances against a possible later British entry into the Community.

To retrace our steps somewhat, the account of imperial preferences does not exhaust the economic aspects of the Commonwealth association. The sterling area, while it includes countries which are not and never have been members of the Commonwealth and does not include Canada which is a member, is nonetheless distinctively associated with the Commonwealth, and Commonwealth members of the sterling bloc have a predominant voice in its management. Overall, the voluntary arrangements constituted by the sterling area have been regarded by Commonwealth members as a useful and cohesive factor. Then there are such matters as United Kingdom investment in Commonwealth countries, for the London money market has special knowledge of Commonwealth conditions. Of course, United Kingdom investment funds for such purposes are limited and go in search of profit, and for countries with ambitious programs of development there are other and often richer sources of aid outside the Commonwealth. As an African nationalist leader has said, with independence the mangoes grow no faster on the mango trees—and it may be, for some time anyway, that they grow less efficiently and even perhaps more slowly.

The United Kingdom has made available economic aid and technical assistance to newly independent Commonwealth countries, and so too have other Commonwealth countries. The Colombo Plan had its genesis in a Commonwealth Foreign Ministers' Conference in 1950. The Plan was originally a Commonwealth scheme to give aid, both through capital and technical assistance, to South and Southeast Asia, and while it remains focused on this area, the Plan has been expanded beyond the Commonwealth in respect both of its donor and donee member states. The United States here, as in so many programs, contributes the preponderant share of aid. At the 1958 Commonwealth Economic Conference at Montreal, Canada announced a program of aid to the West Indies and to other Commonwealth countries not under the Colombo Plan umbrella. In the Report of the Montreal Conference, the theme of Commonwealth interdependence was stressed:

> The economic problems of the Commonwealth reflect . . . differences in economic advancement. But the Commonwealth countries are interdependent in that the progress of each is affected in greater or lesser degree by the prosperity of the others. In particular, the rapid advancement of the less-developed countries is a matter of major concern to their more prosperous partners.

In 1960, at the meeting of the Commonwealth Economic Consultative Council, Commonwealth Finance Ministers initiated a special Commonwealth African Assistance Plan. Its dimensions were modest and largely confined to the provision of technical assistance. It was contemplated that assistance would be given bilaterally and by increased support of existing organizations.

III

Consideration of investment and aid programs within the Commonwealth shows that these are primarily, though not exclusively, arrangements and relationships between the United Kingdom and individual Commonwealth countries.

It is the *London* money market that is the preponderant Commonwealth source of investment; aid schemes are generally *United Kingdom* grants to recently dependent territories to help them along the not infrequently uncomfortable road of independence. And this points up a significant aspect of the Commonwealth relationship which goes far beyond trade and aid. It is well stated by Miller when he says that

> . . . the position of Britain is crucial, since it is with Britain, rather than with one another, that the Commonwealth members have their main contacts. Britain gives more time and energy to the cultivation of the Commonwealth than any other member. . . . Primarily, the Commonwealth is a British interest. Unless it were so, the other members would not join together to carry on the kind of discussion and consultation which they undergo now. What they have in common is that they all wish to preserve the connection with Britain. They have different reasons for this, and there is no point in assuming that their reasons are all the same. . . . But the fact that it is in the interests of each one to continue association with Britain, and in Britain's interests that this should be so, provides a nexus between them strong enough to make them see themselves not simply as engaged in friendly relations with Britain but as connected with one another.[17]

The strength of the bonds between the United Kingdom and individual Commonwealth countries varies, but without these bonds the Commonwealth would surely be meaning-less. And it is interesting to reflect, from an Australian standpoint, how slight can be the connections with Commonwealth countries other than the United Kingdom. To many Australians, the Commonwealth is a comforting but cloudy conception made clear and meaningful only by the articulation and maintenance of links with the United Kingdom. Australian connections with an old Commonwealth associate like Canada are quite tenuous; both countries have important associations with the United Kingdom and the United States but astonishingly few links, particularly personal links, with each other. Australia's bonds with Asian members of the Commonwealth may be stressed for defense and foreign policy reasons, but once again there are very few personal links. Australian migration policies—though they do not impede the movements of students, visitors, and travelers—do not make for easier understanding. And it is also true to say, I think, that in a more general way attitudes to the Commonwealth vary as between its older and its more recent members. To quote a recent commentator:

The Commonwealth occupies a place of pride and honour and affection in the thinking and feeling of the ordinary citizen of the older member states. He may think of it only on rare occasions but when he does, it is usually with pleasure and satisfaction. Who can seriously believe that this is true of the citizens of the new member nations? I can see no reason for deluding ourselves on such a matter.[18]

What then are the bonds of Commonwealth? They are certainly not a common view of foreign policy in a divided world. It is a question though, whether a Communist state, bound up with Communist alliances, could easily remain a member of the Commonwealth. Recent history warns us to be wary of almost any dogmatic propositions touching the Commonwealth, but I think that Miller is right in pointing out that differences in foreign policy within the Commonwealth, sharp though they have been, have not so far encompassed the whole spectrum, and it is hard to see how this association, informal and familial in character and definition, could meaningfully accommodate a Communist state.

We have discussed economic ties, and while their value and importance should not be underestimated they do not of themselves account for the survival of the Commonwealth. Moreoover, they are diminishing in significance and this is likely to be a continuing process. I speak with no authority as an economist, but there appears to be no reality in the prospect, conjured up by some during the Common Market debate, of a Commonwealth economic bloc. What then is this statement in a recent British government paper?

. . . the members are linked together—have agreed to be associated within the Commonwealth—from a common sense of values, from ideals shared . . . they share a political heritage [from the United Kingdom] which, in spite of diversities of race, culture and tradition, has given rise, with local adaptations, to a broadly similar pattern of government.[19]

Such themes occur not infrequently in Commonwealth discourse. President Azikiwe of Nigeria said in 1958 that "we are proud of our British connection because we have been schooled in the art and science of democracy." A year later an Indian participant in a Commonwealth conference wrote:

> . . . when men and women have the same qualifications and codes of conduct, when their minds have been formed upon the same course of reading, when their acquaintance includes friends who have shared the training in other Commonwealth countries, when good faith is fostered by understanding, they cooperate more easily than men and women whose modes of thought, though equally valid in their own circumstances have a different intellectual foundation.

Anyone who travels in the Commonwealth—the new Commonwealth as well as the old—appreciates the force of this point so far as it reflects the existence and continuance of common patterns and traditions in legislative and administrative procedures, in schools and universities, in the professions, and particularly in the legal profession.

Yet too much should not be made of this. Nationalist pressures make for increasing diversity, evidenced for ex-

ample by demands to supplant the English language, and this
generation of new Commonwealth leaders will be followed
by others whose connections with English and English-type
universities and institutions will be more remote. Already,
too, in parts of the new Commonwealth we see evidences of
impatience with doctrines of judicial independence, depress-
ingly highlighted by President Nkrumah's recent dismissal
of the Chief Justice of Ghana for handing down an un-
palatable decision. The trappings, the wigs and gowns, may,
ironically, survive the substance of judicial integrity and
impartiality. And so it is too with governmental institutions:
the parliamentary democracy which established itself in the
United Kingdom was the product of a long, slow process of
historic evolution, and the factors which make for its successful operation in such Commonwealth countries as Australia, New Zealand, and Canada are special—special in the
sense that they do not necessarily appear in other Commonwealth countries with profoundly different histories,
social and economic conditions. We are told by an Indian
commentator that "democracy in India is only a top dressing
on an Indian soil which is essentially undemocratic; caste,
creed, illiteracy and disparities of wealth and social position
all work against its successful and pervasive functioning."
India, conspicuously among the countries of the new Commonwealth, has a genuine commitment to the philosophy
and institutions of parliamentary democracy, but the task of
securing them in that vast and complex country is formi-

dable, almost overwhelming. In Ghana the reality is dictatorship. The catalogue is by no means exhausted by these examples, and it is a depressing one; and we cannot realistically take comfort in the prospect that, in terms of an ultimate democratic achievement, these are cases of taking one step backward to take two forward: *reculer pour mieux sauter*. Of course, one must beware of too many value judgments, but the most cursory survey shows very clearly that a description of Commonwealth countries as sharing a "broadly similar pattern of governmental institutions" is remote from present fact and future prospect. The passing years confirm Miller's judgment in the late 1950's, that it is "impossible to argue that common values and ideals pervade the various societies of the Commonwealth." [20]

The remarkable and rapid growth of Commonwealth membership, bringing together states diverse in race, nationality, religion, culture, size, and importance, has from time to time provoked talk of a "two tier" Commonwealth. As the *London Economist* recently put it, "there has been recurring talk of installing a second row of seats around the Marlborough House table." [21] Marlborough House was recently set aside by Queen Elizabeth as a London site for Commonwealth meetings. The two-tier, second-row proposals point to an organization of an "inner" and "outer" membership and are in part a response to the divisions and differences of outlook between old and new Commonwealth members. The proposals have been deprecated by Commonwealth leaders, who see that the consequence of any such action would be the certain withdrawal of the second tier from the association. But "second tier," "associate member" thinking was also generated by other considerations. Independence has come to many states with almost unbelievable rapidity, and we are reminded that Marlborough House, set aside only a year or two ago for Commonwealth meetings, has only twenty office suites. New members are about to present themselves who will take the score beyond twenty: they include Malta, Nyasaland (Malawi), and Northern Rhodesia (Zambia), the last two emerging as independent states out of the wreckage of the Central African Federation. Then there will be others at the door, despite the call for restraint, urgent in the *cri du coeur* of a member of the British House of Commons in the aftermath of the Zanzibar revolution: "Will the Government promise the House and the country that in future the Union Jack will not be pulled down so easily and so often?" The question gives voice to a well-understood protest, but it will not stem the tide. The question then is: how does one organize an association with a membership of such a size that the familial, informal character of the association can no longer be preserved? Are terms of equal membership appropriate to countries so unequal in population, resource, and significance? A few years ago, there was some talk of associate membership for states of small population and resource. Some are very small indeed. Zanzibar has a population of 325,000 and an *annual* budget less in amount than the *weekly* turnover of a leading English chain store. Trinidad's population is less than one million. As the world goes, no one can say that any size is too small, any demonstration of economic non-viability relevant, in setting criteria for admission to membership. But as a matter of practical politics, proposals for a status of associate member have been quickly abandoned, for there is little enthusiasm for any classification of membership which would blur the simple principle of parity. However, the price must be paid, and I believe that there is a real possibility that growth of this sort will diffuse the Commonwealth into nothingness.

The point is that membership costs nothing. As Mr. Nehru said a decade ago: "Our association with the Commonwealth, novel as it is—for this is a novel way of countries associating with each other—shows a way for future association of nations with each other, without any obligation, without coming in the slightest in the way of each other's independence." This underscores Miller's point that the Commonwealth is best defined as a concert of convenience which allows the members to go their own ways; its very looseness explains why India and Pakistan can co-exist within the Commonwealth. It is only when the policies of a member are unbearably provocative to a substantial segment of Commonwealth opinion that it is difficult to contain it within the Commonwealth mansion. But the only example of this, so far, has been the South African case. Leaders of the new Commonwealth have also stressed positive advantages in membership. To quote again from the same speech of Mr. Nehru:

> I think we have gained positively by being in the Commonwealth. Definitely so. During the past five years especially, many avenues have opened out to us which may not have been opened if we had not been there. I think we have somewhat affected world policies not only directly in so far as we can, but to some extent indirectly also through the Commonwealth, and I think that that is to our and to the world's advantage.

Other contemporary Commonwealth leaders have said very much the same thing. And, as I have suggested earlier, Commonwealth membership has been regarded by small states on attaining independence as "independence with something added and not independence with something taken away," to quote a felicitous phrase of Peter Fraser, then Prime Minister of New Zealand. For the United Kingdom, in a world in which colonialism is fast disappearing and where its survivals meet with relentless, obsessed attack, the Commonwealth—once again to cite the *London Economist*—provides both a gentle letdown to ease the psychological impact of the loss of Empire and also an opportunity to preserve friendship and, in some places, some influence.

Yet one has the sense, in the recent past, that enthusiasm for the Commonwealth is diminishing. This is very much the thrust of Lord Casey's recent book on the future of the Commonwealth in which he argues the desirability of taking more positive action to renew the strength of the association through developing and encouraging various relationships and activities between its members. That this is desirable in the interests of preserving the Commonwealth there can be little doubt, for friendship, as Dr. Johnson admonished, is something that needs to be kept in constant repair. But I do not see, in the vastly expanded contemporary Commonwealth, an association of much enduring significance, for it has ceased, or has largely ceased, to have either coherence or distinctiveness of character. Again, although it may be that individual states choose to go their own way out of the association, I do not see any immediate prospect or threat of formal breakup or dissolution, for there is no constraint or obligation in membership and little to react against. But whatever the future holds, the evolution and development of the Commonwealth has been a notable event in world history, and the association, for some of its members anyway, has had a special significance and meaning arising out of its historic and familial character which no other international association has matched.

NOTES

I. THE EMERGENCE AND DEFINITION OF THE COMMONWEALTH OF NATIONS

1. Underhill, The British Commonwealth, An Experiment in Cooperation among Nations 92–93 (1956).
2. London Economist, May 18, 1963, 633.
3. Schonfeld, *After Brussels,* Foreign Affairs 722 (1963).
4. London Economist, July 14, 1956, 109.
5. Walker, *Policy for the Commonwealth,* in McKetterick and Younger, eds., Fabian International Essays 190–91 (1957).
6. Jennings, Problems of the New Commonwealth 4 (1958); see also Attlee, Empire into Commonwealth 40–41 (Chichele Lectures 1961).
7. Underhill, *op. cit. supra* note 1, at 76.
8. Attlee, *op. cit. supra* note 6, at 18.
9. Magruder, *Commonwealth Status of Puerto Rico,* 15 U. Pitt. L. Rev. 1 (1953).
10. Underhill, *op. cit. supra* note 1, at 6.

11. Walker, *Commonwealth Secretary*, 1 Journal of Commonwealth Political Studies 23–24 (1961).

12. Mansergh, The Multi-Racial Commonwealth 155 (1955).

13. Carrington, *Between the Commonwealth and Europe*, 38 International Affairs 456 (1962).

14. Cited Wheare, The Statute of Westminster and Dominion Status 5–6 (5th ed. 1953).

15. Cited Mansergh, *Commonwealth Membership*, in Mansergh, *et al.*, Commonwealth Perspectives 13 (1958).

16. Hall, *The Genesis of the Balfour Declaration of 1926*, Journal of Commonwealth Studies 169 (1962).

17. [1952] 1 Times Law Reports 1245, 1255.

18. [1926] A.C. 482.

19. Sir Owen Dixon (Chief Justice of Australia) in Copyright Owners' Reproduction Society Ltd. v. E.M.I. (Australia) Pty. Ltd. 100 Commw. L.R. 579, 612 (1958).

20. [1935] A.C. 500, 520.

21. [1952] 1 T.L.R. 1245, 1261.

22. Copyright Owners' Reproduction Society Ltd. v. E.M.I. (Australia) Pty. Ltd. 100 Commw. L.R. 597, 604 (1958).

23. Wheare, The Constitutional Structure of the Commonwealth 88 (1960).

24. Lord Jowitt, (Lord Chancellor) in Attorney-General for Ontario v. Attorney-General for Canada [1947] A.C. 127, 148.

25. Wheare, *op. cit. supra* note 14, at 99.

26. Jennings, Constitutional Problems in Pakistan 191 (1957).

27. Attlee, *op. cit. supra* note 6, at 21.

28. Attorney-General for Ontario v. Attorney-General for Canada [1947] A.C. 153–54.

29. The Judicial Committee of the Privy Council, *Retrospect and Prospect*, Current Legal Problems 5 (1950); see also Camp-

bell, *The Decline of the Jurisdiction of the Privy Council,*
33 Austl. L. J. 196 (1959).

II. THE MULTIRACIAL COMMONWEALTH:
REDEFINITION AND ADJUSTMENT

1. Fawcett, The *Inter Se* Doctrine of Commonwealth Relations 5 (1958).
2. Underhill, The British Commonwealth, An Experiment in Cooperation among Nations 79 (1956).
3. Miller, The Commonwealth in the World 55 (1958).
4. DeSmith, The London Declaration of the Commonwealth Prime Ministers, 12 Modern L. Rev. 351 (1949).
5. Mansergh, *Commonwealth Membership,* in Mansergh, *et al.,* Commonwealth Perspectives 31 (1958).
6. [1955] A.C. 491.
7. Municipal Council of Sydney v. Bull [1909] 1 K.B. 7.
8. See Kahan v. Pakistan Federation [1951] 2 K.B. 1003.
9. See O'Higgins, *The Enahoro Case* 12 Intl. & Comp. L. Q. 1364 (1963); Clute, *Law and Practice in Commonwealth Extradition,* 8 Am. J. Comp. L. 24–28 (1959).
10. [1963] 3 Weekly L. R. 1471.
11. In re Brassey's Settlement; Barclay Bank Ltd. v. Brassey [1955] 1 Weekly L. R. 192.
12. Markwald v. Attorney-General [1920] 1 Chancery Division 348.
13. Cmd. 7326 of 1947. Wilson & Clute, *Commonwealth Citizenship and Common Status,* 57 Am. J. Intl. L. 568 (1963).
14. London Times, November 17, 1961, 19.
15. London Observer, July 15, 1962, 38.
16. [1958] A.C. 301.

17. Wilson & Clute, *op. cit. supra* note 13, at 580–81.
18. Wheare, The Constitutional Structure of the Commonwealth 127 (1960).
19. Miller, *South Africa's Departure*, 1 Journal of Commonwealth Political Studies 56 (1961).
20. Holmes, *The Impact of the Commonwealth on the Emergence of Africa*, 16 International Organization 291 (1962).
21. Miller, *op. cit. supra* note 19, at 70.
22. Lord Ismay in London Daily Telegraph, April 16, 1952.
23. Franks, Britain and the Tide of World Affairs (1955), cited in Underhill, *op. cit. supra* note 2, at 73.
24. Sir Gilbert Laithwaite, Permanent Under Secretary of the Commonwealth Relations Office, in Evidence before a Select Parliamentary Committee cited Miller, The C. R. O., and *Commonwealth Relations*, 2 International Studies (New Delhi) 12 (1960).
25. *Id.* at 56.
26. London Economist, September 22, 1962, 1081.
27. Wheare, *op. cit. supra* note 18, at 146.
28. Underhill, *op. cit. supra* note 2, at 99.
29. Miller, *op. cit. supra* note 3, at 69.
30. Eayrs, *Canadian Policy and Opinion During the Suez Crisis*, 12 International Journal 97 (1957).

III. THE POLITICS AND PROSPECTS OF THE CONTEMPORARY COMMONWEALTH

1. Mansergh, *Commonwealth Foreign Policies* in Commonwealth Perspectives 58 (1958).
2. Moore, Constitution of the Commonwealth of Australia 301 (2nd ed. 1910).
3. Commonwealth v. New South Wales 32 Commw. L. R. 200, 208 (1923).

4. Cowen, Australia and the United States, Some Legal Comparisons 27 (1954).

5. See Wilson, *The Commonwealth and the Law of Nations,* in Mansergh, *et al.,* Commonwealth Perspectives 74–75 (1958).

6. See Watt, *Imperial Defence Policy and Imperial Foreign Policy 1911–1939, A Neglected Paradox,* 1 Journal of Commonwealth Political Studies 266 (1963).

7. Cited Mansergh, The Commonwealth and the Nations 79 (1948).

8. Fawcett, *The Commonwealth in the United Nations,* 1 Journal of Commonwealth Political Studies 134 (1962).

9. Mansergh, The Multi-Racial Commonwealth 138 (1955).

10. *Id.* at 44.

11. See McHenry and Rosecrance, *The Exclusion of the United Kingdom from the ANZUS Pact,* 12 International Organization 320 (1958).

12. Underhill, The British Commonwealth, An Experiment in Cooperation among Nations 20 (1956).

13. Central Office of Information, Consultation and Cooperation in the Commonwealth 17 (1961).

14. Miller, The Commonwealth in the World 263 (1958).

15. Casey, The Future of the Commonwealth 144 (1963).

16. *Id.* at 36.

17. Miller, *op. cit. supra* note 14, at 252, 260.

18. W. H. Morris-Jones in a paper to the Indian Council of World Affairs, New Delhi, March 18, 1960, cited Casey, *op. cit. supra* note 15, at 23.

19. Central Office of Information, What Is the Commonwealth 7 (1962).

20. Miller, *op. cit. supra* note 14, at 260.

21. London Economist, January 11, 1964, 93.

PUBLISHED ROSENTHAL
LECTURES 1949–1965

1948 Hazard, John N. "The Soviet Union and International Law," *Illinois Law Review*, XLIII, 591.

1949 Freund, Paul A. *On Understanding the Supreme Court.* Boston: Little, Brown & Co.

1951 Dawson, John P. *Unjust Enrichment, A Comparative Analysis.* Boston: Little, Brown & Co.

1952 Feller, Abraham H. *United Nations and World Community.* Boston: Little, Brown & Co.

1952 Horsky, Charles A. *The Washington Lawyer.* Boston: Little, Brown & Co.

1953 Vanderbilt, Arthur T. "The Essentials of A Sound Judicial System," *Northwestern University Law Review*, XLVIII.

1954 Berle, Adolf A., Jr. *The Twentieth Century Capitalist Revolution.* New York: Harcourt, Brace.

1956 Hurst, James W. *Law and the Conditions of Freedom in the Nineteenth Century United States.* Madison: University of Wisconsin Press.

1956 Sohn, Louis B. "United Nations Charter Revision and the Rule of Law: A Program for Peace," *Northwestern University Law Review*, L, 709.

1956   Gross, Ernest A. "Major Problems in Disarmament,"
        Northwestern University Law Review, LI, 299.

1956   Parker, John J. "Dual Sovereignty and the Federal
        Courts," *Northwestern University Law Review*, LI, 407.

1957   Ukai, Nobushige. "The Individual and the Rule of Law
        Under the New Japanese Constitution," *Northwestern
        University Law Review*, LI, 733.

1957   Papale, Antonia Edward. "Judicial Enforcement of De-
        segregation: Its Problems and Limitations," *Northwest-
        ern University Law Review*, LII, 301.

1957   Hart, Herbert L.A. "Murder and the Principles of Punish-
        ment: England and the United States," *Northwestern
        University Law Review*, LII, 433.

1958   Green, Leon. *Traffic Victims: Tort Law and Insurance.*
        Evanston, Ill.: Northwestern University Press.

1960   Radcliffe, Cyril John. *The Law and Its Compass.* Evanston,
        Ill.: Northwestern University Press.

1961   Eisenstein, Louis. *The Ideologies of Taxation.* New York:
        Ronald Press.

1961   Havighurst, Harold C. *The Nature of Private Contract.*
        Evanston, Ill.: Northwestern University Press.

1962   Pike, James Albert. *Beyond the Law:* the religious and
        ethical meaning of the lawyer's vocation. New York:
        Doubleday and Co.

1964   Katz, Wilber G. *Religion and American Constitutions.*
        Evanston, Ill.: Northwestern University Press.

1965   Cowen, Zelman. *The British Commonwealth of Nations
        in a Changing World:* law, politics, and prospects.
        Evanston, Ill.: Northwestern University Press.

A NOTE ON MANUFACTURE

THE TEXT OF THIS BOOK was set on the Linotype in a face called JANSON, an "Old Face" of the Dutch school cut in Amsterdam by the Hungarian, Nicholas Kis, *circa* 1690. *Janson's* authorship was long attributed erroneously to Anton Janson, a Hollander who had been employed in Leipzig where the matrices were re-discovered. These same mats are today in the possession of the Stempel foundry, Frankfurt, and the machine-cast version you are reading was modelled directly on type produced from the original strikes.

The book was composed, printed, and bound by KINGS-PORT PRESS, INC., Kingsport, Tennessee. WARREN PAPER COMPANY manufactured the paper.